Strategic Decisions and Weak Signals

FOCUS SERIES

Series Editor Jean-Charles Pomerol

Strategic Decisions and Weak Signals

Anticipation for Decision-Making

Humbert Lesca
Nicolas Lesca

WILEY

First published 2014 in Great Britain and the United States by ISTE Ltd and John Wiley & Sons, Inc.

ISTE Ltd
27-37 St George's Road
London SW19 4EU
UK

www.iste.co.uk

John Wiley & Sons, Inc.
111 River Street
Hoboken, NJ 07030
USA

www.wiley.com

Library of Congress Control Number: 2014934505

British Library Cataloguing-in-Publication Data
A CIP record for this book is available from the British Library
ISSN 2051-2481 (Print)
ISSN 2051-249X (Online)
ISBN 978-1-84821-609-9

Printed and bound in Great Britain by CPI Group (UK) Ltd., Croydon, Surrey CR0 4YY

Contents

Introduction

VERBATIM I.1.– (transcription of recordings made during consultancy visits to organizations).–

"How can we detect any potential weak signals within big volumes of digital data? How do we interpret the weak signals thus brought to light? How can we train people in the organization to perform this type of task?"

In other words, the question is "What actionable knowledge (methods and computer-based techniques) would you recommend for serving the aforementioned purposes?"

I.1. Anticipative strategic scanning

The study of the exploitation of weak signals in organizational strategy is a challenging business, and one which has only been being practiced in organizations surprisingly recently. The concepts involved are relatively numerous, and the definitions given for such concepts may well vary from one author to the other. The real-world application of these concepts is rarely touched upon in the existing body of literature, and this gaping lacuna is a hindrance to the development of *anticipative strategic scanning*, in commercial companies and public organizations.

Therefore, this book aims to introduce working methods and computer-based systems to facilitate experimentation and operational implementation. Chapter 2 of the book presents the state of the art on the topic, gleaned from the publications of academic researchers. Chapter 3 then gives a presentation of three operational systems and looks at the case studies for their application.

The "scanning" of an organization's environment to aid in *strategic decision-making* is not really a new idea. The precursor was, undoubtedly, set by F. Aguilar, with his book *Scanning the Business Environment*, which was published in 1967 [AGU 67]. Then, after a period of relative silence on the subject, a clutch of articles and books were published around the early 1980s, such as *Managing Strategic Surprise by Response to Weak Signals* by H.I. Ansoff in 1975 [ANS 75]. Thereafter, there were few new publications on the subject until the late 1990s. A new wave of publications began in the early 2000s and has continued steadily ever since. One of the major reasons for this is the rapid progress of online data-mining technology.

Paradoxically, "environmental scanning" and anticipative strategic scanning have not yet become as widely used in companies as might be suggested by the high number of academic publications on the subject. The explanation for this paradox probably lies in the following two facts:

– The considerable progress in information-seeking technology has led to a real problem of *information overload* both in private enterprises and public organizations; managers are rarely well prepared for *anticipative scanning* of the business environment.

– There is, as we have just seen, an over-abundance of raw information (data), but techniques to *make sense* of these data are not progressing at the same rate, leading to situations of *information overload*. Furthermore, in the area of education, practically no institutions or universities have introduced training courses in the area of anticipative strategic scanning and the use of weak signals in strategic decision-making.

At present, the techniques for mining raw data are continuing to progress faster than techniques and expertise (particularly those relating to the detection and interpretation of weak signals). However, we have clearly seen a proliferation in demand from managers on the ground, including those formulated above or those expressed by the *verbatim quotes* peppered throughout the chapters. It is this demand that this book aims to satisfy.

I.2. Acknowledgments

The innovative systems presented in Chapter 3 are the product of doctoral research projects conducted at the Centre d'Etudes et de Recherches Appliquées à la Gestion (CERAG), at the university of Grenoble-Alpes, France. Edison Loza Aguirre worked on the TARGETBUILDER project, Alex Buitrago worked on the APROXIMA project and Annette Casagrande worked on the ALHENA project. The authors would like to express their heartfelt thanks and their best wishes for these researchers' work in the future.

The Subject within the Field of Management Science: Concepts and Issues

Management science aims to help managers in making decisions. Such decisions include information of a strategic nature, and they are the basis of "strategic management". Decision-making relies, notably, on the use of relevant information. This information is itself produced by an information system (or several such systems). Hence, strategic management of an organization and the management of the information systems are highly interdependent. The interplay between these two fields is illustrated in Figure 1.1.

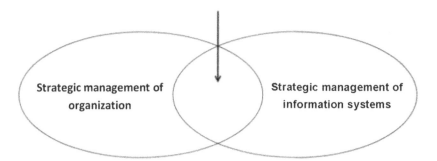

Figure 1.1. *Field of investigation*

A number of authors have looked into the characteristics of information systems for strategic management. One such author is D.C. Bernhardt, who expresses what managers want thus: "I want it fast, factual, actionable" [BER 94].

More recently, Xu *et al.* [XU 11] conducted a survey of UK executives. "Three focus group sessions were conducted with a total of 31 middle and top-level executives [...] Most of the participants are at strategic (48%) level and tactical level (39%) and involved in some forms of executive intelligence activities. Each session began with a brief statement on the rationale and objectives, the confidentiality and ground rules for the discussion (e.g. role of moderator, one participant talks at a time and disagreement is welcomed), and the demonstration of the visualization model. Focus group sessions took about an hour to complete. The focus group discussion allows taping [*sic.*] into human tendencies" [XU 11, p. 192].

What information about the organization's environment do executives want when making a strategic decision? The following results give us a clue:

– "Executives are busy with other activities and have limited time and capacity to scan all possible information, thus an automated information scanning agent may be perceived useful by executives.

– Scanning without filtering could lead to over-abundance of irrelevant information that exacerbates the problem of data overload... On the other hand, executives raised concerns on the possibility of screening out potentially relevant information.

– It is assumed that alerting as a result of intelligent scanning is vital to keep executive instantly informed about strategic issues, thus, is essential to turn the agent system into a vigilant system for executives. Executives may perceive this function useful" [XU 11, p. 193].

1.1. Strategic management and strategic decision-making

Organizational strategy is of prime importance in management science. The word "strategic" may refer to one of two things: the *decision-making process* whereby a strategic plan is drawn up as a guide to action or the actual implementation of the strategic plan on the ground (the "roadmap"). In both cases, time is of the essence: it takes time to draw up a strategic plan, and the action may take place in future years and, therefore, over the course of several or even many years. Anticipation is therefore a prerequisite.

Figure 1.2. *Strategic decision-making is at the heart of strategic management*

One of the main questions that managers (likely) ask themselves is: "What is the strength of my organization today? What will it be tomorrow?". The answer to this question sheds light on the area in which the manager needs to make the decisions that are vital for the success of the organization both at present and in the *future*.

A strategic strength for today may well no longer be as strategically important tomorrow. It is therefore vital to detect, as early as possible, any drivers of change that might emerge in the organization's environment, and the *signs* that herald these changes, in order to be able to take account of them in strategic decision-making. Exaggerating somewhat, we might say: "Tell me the 'driving forces' behind your organization and I will tell you what the key information is which your organization absolutely must research on the subject of the (internal and external) changes for which it needs to be prepared if you want sustainable competitiveness". Such information is gleaned from an *information system* for strategic management.

In preparing this book, we conducted interviews with numerous managers; verbatim quotes are given throughout the book. Some managers stated that they were not overly concerned by environmental scanning as such: the *environment* is, in their eyes, too fuzzy a notion to be truly motivating. On the other hand, those same managers appeared more motivated by the notion of a *project*.

EXAMPLE 1.1.– (Petrobras)

"There are many, many challenges at the moment... but we are beginning to see the effects of a completely pragmatic, project-based policy" [THE 13].

As soon as the desire to conduct a project emerges, such managers seek to gather the useful information to facilitate the implementation of that project. The concept of a project is therefore important in terms of triggering and structuring environmental scanning. Nevertheless, it gives us only a partial answer to the question at hand. Indeed, when a project surfaces, it becomes easier to see what information needs to be gathered, but in order to get to this point, environmental scanning needs to be performed first, so as to detect opportunities for projects. Two cases must therefore be distinguished:

– it is the desire to conduct a project that triggers the act of environmental scanning;

– it is the discovery of opportunities that triggers the desire to conduct a project.

The delimitation of the field of environmental scanning is not obvious; it arises from a choice rather than from a prerequisite. Each organization needs to reflect on what it deems important to scan in order to feed into its strategic thinking, and that choice is, in itself, a *strategic decision*. Yet this choice may not always be made in a methodical manner.

In fact, there are two dangers which the organization needs to consider:

– the organization collects too little information because it is scanning too limited an environment: it is blind to possible opportunities or risks;

– the organization collects too much information about its environment. Thus, it is paralyzed by information overload, with potentially useless information; this information overload can, itself, give rise to blindness and paralysis.

VERBATIM 1.1.– (industrial sectors)

"We do not go looking for information. We content ourselves with the information that comes to us."

"We do not have any sort of organized system with regard to anticipative environmental scanning. Certainly, pieces of information are given by one person or another, but without a specific goal, on a case-by-case basis, depending on each individual's perception of matters."

"We have a great deal of information, but it always reaches us too late. I'm constantly running to catch up with things that have already happened."

"We have a great many information circuits, but for day-to-day information. If a piece of information which acts as an early warning signal for a genuine change in the environment is channeled along one of those circuits, there is a high chance of it being lost."

1.2. Strategic decision-making and anticipation

Strategic decision-making and anticipation should, logically, be very closely bound together: "[...] environmental scanning is integrally linked to organizational and strategic planning and plans for unexpected changes that will affect the organization" [ALB 04, p. 41].

Strategic decision-making

Figure 1.3. *Anticipation is at the heart of strategic decision-making*

1.2.1. *Knowing and anticipating*

A *condition sine qua non*, when initiating a new strategy, is *knowing* the relevant environment and *anticipating* evolution of that environment. This involves anticipating in order to:

– trigger the desire to make a strategic decision;

– develop a plan of the process whereby the chosen decision is implemented.

The *external environment* in which the strategic decision needs to be made and implemented is:

– complex, comprising numerous elements;

– rapidly changing [EIS 88];

– equivocal [DAF 86];

– nonlinear [WAL 92].

Ultimately, we speak of turbulence and uncertainty.

VERBATIM 1.2.– (AXA Insurance)

"Increasingly, we are having to anticipate in terms of our competitors, new banking technology, lobby groups, associations, federations, and even the new national and international regulations, etc."

"Organizations today face unprecedented challenges in maintaining commercial survival and success. *Success requires a keen strategic understanding of external influences in order to respond in ways that will ensure the organization's survival and success*" [ALB 04, p. 39]. On this point, the manager's attitude is of crucial importance.

EXAMPLE 1.2.– (survey put to 309 managers in the United States) [QIU 08]

The survey shows that scanning of the organization's relevant environment depends primarily on the attitude of the managers. The organization's competitive intelligence is greater when the managers have a proactive attitude, driven by the will to find a representation that clarifies the opportunities and threats in the environment in order to be able to respond to them quickly.

What marks the difference between the attitudes of two managers with regard to *managerial scanning behavior*? Two major aspects are held up in the literature:

– the *scope* of the field observed;

– the *frequency* of observation.

We will come back to these concepts later on.

These three periods, anticipating, deciding and implementing, are of different durations. The third period, which is generally the longest, may be carried out over several or even many years.

1.2.2. *Anticipating and deciding*

With regard to the total lifetime of a strategic decision, we can distinguish three periods:

– The first is the period where the decision has not yet been made, but the decision-making project is in the pipeline, and it will ultimately trigger the decision-making process. The exploitation of weak signals may be useful in envisioning a future strategy. This weak signal may be useful in designing a future strategy. This initial exploitation is generally ignored in the existing literature.

– The second is the period where the decision is elaborated and the plan of action is established.

– The third is the period where the decision is implemented. It may be useful to exploit weak signals to drive forward the application of the strategy to a fruitful end.

1.2.2.1. *Triggering*

Triggering is the arousal of the desire to move toward a new strategy. In general, the act of environmental scanning and anticipation of any evolution in the environment will trigger the perception that it is opportune to make a decision: "The prerequisite for dynamic business planning is to capture this *unknown*" [ILM 06, p. 909].

Anticipation is a necessary condition, depending on the case, for reactivity or proactivity: "[...] then distinguish between two types of early warning systems (EWSs): (1) proactive, in which an organisation first determines which issues it finds important and then goes about monitoring those issues; (2) reactive, in which an organisation uses the EWS as a radar looking for unexpected changes" [BOT 10, p. 457].

"The term 'agile' is commonly used to describe firms that are able to adapt and to perform well in rapidly changing environments... enterprise agility, that is, the ability of firms to sense environmental change and respond readily, is an important determinant of firm success... As a result, enterprise agility is best viewed as applying to episodic events precipitated by environmental change, whereas absorptive capacity operates on a more continuous basis" [OVE 06, p. 120].

EXAMPLE 1.3.–

In Germany in 2013, more than *180 universities* and *120 research centers and institutes* were engaged in research regarding *Energiewende*, Germany's transition to a more sustainable form of energy supply. The Federal Ministry of Education and Research, on 4 March 2013, announced the creation of a national research platform on *Energiewende*. The aims were, notably, to bring together existing activities and new projects, to make knowledge available to all, and thereby *"identify"* *new important topics in time* and *be able to react quickly* [BUL 13].

1.2.2.2. *Planning*

Planning entails preparing the plan of action that will facilitate the new strategy's implementation.

The development of the *plan of action* varies depending on the intended strategic objective: to adapt or to create.

1.2.2.2.1. Adapting to the anticipated future

It is necessary to procure anticipative information as the basis upon which to construct an image of the future, resulting from the processing of the gathered data. The approach then involves revealing (in the photographic sense of the word) the image of the future in order to prepare the organization to be able to adapt to it. The organization must prove itself to be *reactive* and adaptable and, in order to do so, scan its environment.

EXAMPLE 1.4.– (justice sector) [BOT 10]

In this particular case, the *strategic decisions* in question are those taken by the *Dutch Ministry of Justice*. The objectives envisioned are long-term objectives (over 20 years or so), and the environment will undoubtedly change over the years, but it is impossible to predict in exactly what way. "Looking to the future is not just a matter of exploring future trends (i.e. changes over time) but also of detecting current signals or events that may announce a change or shift in existing trends. Early warning systems (EWS) are used to detect and identify these seeds of change that can even develop into discontinuities" [BOT 10, p. 457].

EWS denotes a device that is able *to detect any differences between the evolution of the environment and the implementation of the strategy* and trigger a *warning signal to take corrective action.* A warning signal lies in a difference between an aspect "measured" at a given point in time and the situation that was predicted in the "trend" (or strategic plan or roadmap) for the same date. This difference may signify a possible shift in circumstances, liable to lead to the failure of the policy desired and implemented by the strategic decisions made by the Ministry. In such a case, the difference is referred to as a *weak signal* [BOT 10, p. 458].

Once detected, the signal needs to be interpreted: "How do we know to which signals we need to pay attention?" The interpretation arrived at becomes the *trigger* for "incremental" corrective measures, in order to remain on the path leading from the initial situation to the final situation intended by the Ministry. "This creates a path to the future with which the sustainability of (new) policies can be tested periodically" [BOT 10, p. 454].

1.2.2.2.2. Shaping one's own future

To create the future as the organization wants it to be, it is necessary to obtain the anticipative information that will help to envisage the probable environment wherein the organization needs to "impose" the place and the role it deliberately wishes to play: What do we want to become? What do we want to be the first to do? What innovation is necessary for us to shake off all competitors? In this case, the organization needs to show itself to be *proactive*.

EXAMPLE 1.5.– (Ministry of Economic Affairs)

Lin *et al.* [LIN 12] present an example of a process of anticipation by the *Ministry of Economic Affairs* in Taiwan with a view to shaping its own future.

In the late 1990s, the Ministry itself set a very ambitious project corresponding to the following strategic vision: to become a world leader in the chosen technological field (electronic and computing industries) by 2020.

The goal, here, is not to adapt to such changes in the environment as may be predicted at the time of preparation of the decision (reactive behavior) but rather to create the vision of the future chosen as an objective, i.e. to create a situation which will be radically different by the chosen time – 2020 (proactive behavior). The objective is to make an economic and technological leap to arrive at a situation which is a rupture from the present one.

"The development of Taiwanese industries has changed from an early labor-intensive stage to a later capital-intensive stage, and transformed successfully from a least-developed economy to a developing national economy [...]. In the 1980s, Taiwan established an ICT leading position through R&D on science and technology with ICT and electronic industries as the leading industries. Confronting the knowledge economy in the 21st Century, Taiwan must revolutionize its national future development strategies and directions" [LIN 12, p. 1586].

Depending on whether the organization has opted for reactivity or proactivity, the information needing to be gathered is different. We will go into further detail about the difference later on.

1.2.3. *Anticipating for effective decision-making*

Once the type of strategy has been chosen and the "roadmap" for that strategy is drawn up, it needs to be implemented. The exploitation of weak signals may be useful in bringing the strategy to fruition: the need for RADAR may be felt. Often, authors in the pre-existing body of literature have mentioned only this second use of weak signals.

"Once robust strategies have been formulated, the organization is ready to devise scanning and monitoring frameworks to track how the future is unfolding and whether elements of the strategy need to be fine-tuned or perhaps fundamentally revised. This is one main purpose of the strategic radar in our model, as described..." [SCH 13a, p. 818].

1.2.3.1. *Anticipating to choose the right moment*

The questions are: what information needs to be gathered to successfully implement the strategy and avoid the pitfalls?; which sources should be consulted in order to obtain such information?; will the information mainly be drawn from the ground, or will it be mainly digital data, to be found using the Internet, for example?

1.2.3.2. *Implementing the chosen strategic plan when the time comes*

When the time of triggering comes, the *execution* of the decision begins. The organization then needs to perform the operations, and not deviate from the chosen path, while taking account of what may happen in the future. This is the duty of the *person in charge* of the execution.

EXAMPLE 1.6.– (tourism sector) [PAR 13]

This example relates to the tourism sector in Greece. The authors, Paraskevas and Altinay, present an example of a device to detect an oncoming crisis as early as possible. The first line of defense against the coming crisis lies in the detection of signals indicating it (crisis signals). "Crisis signal detection is acknowledged as an organization's first line of defence" [PAR 13, p. 167]. Then, a solution must be found to deal with the crisis.

Ship metaphor.– Navigating the path from the making of the strategic decision to the ultimate realization of the targeted strategic objective can be compared to piloting a ship whose goal is to reach its destination port: the objective is determined, and the roadmap is represented on the sea chart. Yet during the journey, there is a danger of encountering an unforeseen obstacle: an iceberg, a floating object capable of sinking the ship, a storm, etc. It is therefore imperative to scan the seas around you. To react in time, the captain uses not only the signals that give him/her radar data but also his/her own eyes. When navigating, we have to anticipate in order to be reactive. An unfortunately familiar counter-example is that of the cruise ship "Costa Concordia", which grounded itself on an islet in the Gulf of Naples.

During the three steps – choice of a strategy, development of a roadmap to construct the strategy and operations to implement that strategy – it is necessary to remain alert, to "look forward", to look to the future; to harvest the information needed to anticipate not only obstacles and threats but also opportunities which might be seized; to check the concordance or discordance between the strategic objectives initially chosen and the events likely to arise in the organization's environment; and to compare the lessons drawn from interpretation of the harvested information against the strategic plan. "However, what happens if the vision and the products are not coherent with the future?" In the case in point, the authors specify: "In our opinion, *foresight* has a double aim in the company: to feed *innovation and research* and to strategically guide decision-making and planning" [BAT 11, p. 1030].

Anticipating gives rise to certain needs for managers: needs for appropriate concepts, methods and systems. "In the domain of futures studies, the need to develop methods and concepts to identify risks or opportunities 'early enough' (early detection) has become an issue and almost a discrete sub-field with its own debates, specialties and schools of thought" [ROS 11, p. 375].

Remember that this chapter relates to concepts and the issues raised by their implementation; methods and systems will be dealt with in Chapters 2 and 3.

1.2.4. *Characteristics of a strategic decision*

Anticipating is more than simply extrapolating the past. The word "strategic", when applied to a decision concerning the management of an organization, means that the *decision* has the following characteristics:

– It is made in a situation of uncertainty, with incomplete information, in a complex environment, which is variable or constantly mutating (contrary to "all other things being equal").

– It is never exactly the same on any two occasions, which is a relative handicap for the decision-maker.

– It is made for the longer term: it generally relates to a number of years to come (or even several decades – e.g. with airlines or maritime operators).

– It is likely to have far-reaching consequences (either good or bad), which may endanger the organization's very existence.

– It is systemic (comprising numerous elements with numerous inter-relations).

– The decision-maker has no tried-and-tested models available (it is impossible to use the so-called "turnkey" software).

– "The dynamic properties arising [are] not simply from the interaction of identifiable component systems but from the field itself (the 'ground'). We call these environments turbulent fields. The turbulence results from the complexity and multiple character of the causal interconnections [...]"

[EME 65, p. 19]. In addition, the *choice of time* to make the decision and, in particular, to implement it may be of crucial importance for the success of that decision.

1.3. Anticipation, anticipative information and weak signals

A wide variety of terms are used by the authors in the field: raw data, information, weak signal, early warning signal, anticipative information and capability information. It is necessary to specify the exact meaning of each of these terms. For instance, the term "raw data" is not, in the eyes of specialists, information *per se*. It is a piece of "information" we receive without wanting it, and which is of *no use* to the organization receiving it. "Information", on the other hand, is data which are useful for the receiver. Therefore, it is deservedly qualified as "information".

Figure 1.4. *Weak signals are at the heart of anticipation*

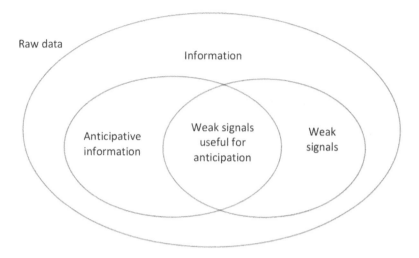

Figure 1.5. *Relative position of the concepts employed*

1.3.1. *Weak signals*

1.3.1.1. *Definition*

A weak signal is a piece of data that usually appears insignificant, or is swamped in a sea of raw data, which generated "noise". It is difficult to perceive, because it does not, *a priori*, impose itself; therefore, it is qualified as "weak". If it catches our attention, it then assumes the status of information.

The concept of a weak signal is sometimes spoken of using different terminology by different authors, and thus assumes subtly different meanings, as Kuusi and Hiltunen [KUU 11] note: "the key feature of the weak signal is that it has *rival* interpretations" [KUU 11, p. 48]. Table 1.1 shows some of the definitions used in existing publications.

Hiltunen points out that a "weak signal" is sometimes spoken of instead as a "wild card" [HIL 06].

Reference	Definition
Ansoff [ANS 75]	"We might call this graduated response through amplification and response to weak signals, in contrast to conventional strategic planning that depends on strong signals. Such a practical method for planning a graduated response can be developed" [p. 23]. "Our expansion has been to admit weak signals as a basis of decision making, and the extension was from a purely planning to a total action system" [p. 32].
Schoemaker *et al.* [SCH 13a]	"Weak signals are defined here as seemingly random or *disconnected pieces of information* that at first appear to be background noise but which can be recognized as part of a larger pattern when viewed through a different frame or by connecting it with other pieces of information." [p. 815]
Ilmola and Kuusi [ILM 06]	"A weak signal is by definition *unstructured* information and its implications to the organization are at an early stage very hard to define. A weak signal represents potential discontinuity, something that the organization has not interpreted before [...] The prerequisite for dynamic business planning is to capture this *unknown* regarding strategic options" [p. 911].
Hiltunen [HIL 07]	"In this study, weak signals mean today's information that can foretell the changes *in the future*. This information might sound funny or strange and it can cause confusion, because it offers a totally new way of thinking/idea/innovation. As time passes, it might come out that weak signals were the first signs or symptoms of a big change, even megatrends. However, weak signals are not always clues about big changes. They might simply be information about strange things that have happened. A practical example of weak signals is an article about some new technical innovation in a magazine" [p. 41].
Schoemaker and Day [SCH 09]	"Among the most well-established of those traps are the biases that underlie how information is filtered, interpreted and often bolstered. The net effect of these biases is that we frame a complex or *ambiguous* issue in a certain way – without fully appreciating other possible perspectives – and then become overconfident about that particular view" [p. 44].

Kuosa 2011 [KUO 11]	"The concept of weak signals refers to observations of the surrounding world which someone has subjectively reasoned to have some special foresight value. In this paper the concept is understood in a broader view. Weak signals can include any qualitative and somehow *surprising* observation of the world which helps us to manage the patterns of chance. The weak signals can be attached to existing or emerging patterns or it can be used to invent a certain pattern. They can sometimes be used for reasoning potentially *emerging patterns* as well. However, it should be noticed that the value of one single signal should not be over emphasized in foresighting. The reasoning of emergence of a certain pattern requires clustering of many different types of patterns" [p. 463].
Yoon [YOO 12]	"This paper considers weak signals as emerging topics related to the keywords that are not much interpreted by people. For example, if the increasing rate of the occurrence frequency of a keyword is peculiar, then the keyword is strongly related to current oddities and strange issues. However, if the keyword has been rarely exposed to people, it is likely to be connected to weak signals" [p. 12544].

Table 1.1. *Definitions for "weak signals" given by various authors*

1.3.1.2. *Outward appearance*

A weak signal may be found in a short fragment of text, a notice, an image, a photo, an overheard remark, etc.: "visual weak signals are weak signals shown in a *visual form*. They can be represented as *images*: photos, paintings, drawings, video clips, etc." [HEI 12, p. 249]. It may also lie in a physical sensation: "weak signals can be perceived through all five human senses: they can be seen, heard, smelled, felt or even tasted" [HEI 12, p. 249].

1.3.2. *Characteristics of a weak signal*

Table 1.2 gives an overview of the characteristics of a weak signal. These characteristics make us to understand that detecting a weak signal is not an easy task.

"Weak" because it is...	Reason for the word "weak"
Fragmentary	The information is incomplete.
Swamped in an ocean of raw data	The weak signal is likely to go unseen by most observers.
Ambiguous or equivocal, meaning unclear	The information may be interpreted in a number of different ways.
Unusual, unfamiliar, unexpected	We are not expecting this signal to occur and are therefore not looking for it, so we may well not see it.
Apparently *useless or unnecessary*	It has no obvious connection to any current concern. The same weak signal may seize the attention of one person but appear devoid of interest to those around him/her. Its usefulness is not immediately apparent.
Uncertain	Its apparently limited reliability means it is not hugely credible.
Unsettling, worrying	An unexpected smell can sometimes constitute a weak signal: e.g. during a visit to an industrial site...
Isolated	We cannot immediately tell which issue to attach the signal to, or what use can be made of it.
Random, erratic	It is meaningless to speak of its frequency of apparition.

Table 1.2. *Some characteristics of a weak signal*

Such characteristics explain why it is useful to gather several weak signals in order to improve their reliability and make sense of them.

VERBATIM 1.3.– (French Ministry of the Economy)

"Everyone is burdened by a mass of fragmentary data which, when viewed separately, are of little interest. It is the combination of those data fragments, and the interpretation we make of them, which is important..."

The necessity to combine weak signals in this way justifies the Puzzle method presented in Chapter 2.

1.3.3. *Weak signals for anticipation*

A weak signal, in spite of its fragile appearance, can alert us to a possible future. Such is the case when our interpretation of weak signals leads us to believe that an event likely to have consequences (in terms of risk, threat or opportunity) may be *shaping to happen (in the future)*. Weak signals are anticipative in nature, because they help us to anticipate: they constitute a warning. Some authors also speak of "early signs" or "early signals", "weak signs", "early warning signs" and "early warning signals".

The dilemma caused by the variation in terminology used for very similar concepts led Kuusi and Hiltunen [KUU 11] to propose the concept of a "future-oriented signification", based on the signification process, which is analyzed from the perspective of three aspects: "signal, interpretation and issue" [KUU 11, p. 47]

In this book, we will use the expression "weak signal".

Reference	Definition
Hiltunen [HIL 07]	"... weak signals mean today's information that can foretell the changes *in the future*. This information might sound funny or strange and it can cause confusion, because it offers a totally new way of thinking/idea/innovation. As time passes, it might come out that weak signals were the first signs or symptoms of a big change, even megatrends. However, weak signals are not always clues about big changes. They might simply be information about strange things that have happened." [p. 2]
Hiltunen [HIL 08]	"weak signals mean today's information than can foretell the changes *in the future*" [p. 21]
Kuosa [KUO 11]	"The concept of weak signals refers to observations of the surrounding world which someone has subjectively reasoned to have some special foresight value [...]. Weak signals can include any qualitative and somehow *surprising* observation of the world which helps us to manage the patterns of chance. The weak signals can be attached to existing or emerging patterns or it can be used to invent a certain pattern. They can sometimes be used for reasoning potentially *emerging patterns* as well. However, it should be noticed that the value of one single signal should not be over emphasized in *foresighting*. The reasoning of emergence of a certain pattern requires clustering of many different types of patterns." [p. 463]
Rossel 2012 [ROS 12]	"The weak signals are *perceptions of possible changes* that are essentially 'candidate' (or hypotheses) within a socially relevant and resonant knowledge building process, that in all cases need to be: 1) conjugated with other weak or strong signal candidates and iteratively matched against change models (a scenario minded step), 2) confronted to one's own bias-producing capabilities, 3) interacted upon with others stakeholders, hopefully involving a diversity of viewpoints, and 4) followed-up and evaluated in light of actual developments, with constant 'early' sensitivity." [p. 236]

Table 1.3. *Anticipative nature mentioned by various authors*

1.3.4. *Where might we find a weak signal?*

A weak signal may, notably, be contained in an *unusual association*:

– between two words in the same sentence;

– between two sentences in the same text;

– between a visual observation and the place where it occurs;

– between a person and the place where he/she was seen;

– and so on.

In all these cases, the weak signal does not appear as such. It is revealed by the reaction of surprise to the unusual nature of the association. It is therefore interesting to know whether there is a means of discovering such associations. We will return to this point in Chapter 3.

EXAMPLE 1.7.–

Here is a press cutting: "*Surprise* resignation of the CEO of the Swiss giant ABB Group [...] The news has taken all analysts entirely by surprise [...] During his 'reign', Joe Hogan increased the corporation's turnover from 35 billion to 39.3 billion dollars" [OGI 13].

For certain readers, the *weak signal* lies in the association between "Joe Hogan was extremely successful during his tenure" and "*Surprise* resignation of the CEO". It is probable (though not certain) that this weak signal will be seen as anticipative by anybody interested in either the actor "Joe Hogan" or the actor "ABB Group".

A weak signal may also lie in the *absence* of information where it would be expected: the mutism of a speech or text may be highly "communicative" for someone who knows how to detect weak signals.

In addition, something that constitutes an anticipative weak signal for one person may be nothing more than raw data for someone else.

EXAMPLE 1.8.–

The newspapers in most countries (in April 2013) carried the news that "President OBAMA [had] decided that WIFI should be free for everyone" (the news was also broadcast by radio stations in many languages). Is this a weak signal or a piece of raw data devoid of interest?

– For most readers, the story was "raw data"; for others, it was "information".

– Yet for some readers, it was also a weak signal because it could suggest a number of consequences that are difficult to specify, but are plausible, and some of which could constitute a social revolution in the United States (as is happening in China, for example).

Weak signal detection requires a mind trained in this type of exercise, and probably an appropriate cognitive style.

1.3.5. *Usefulness of weak signals in strategic decision-making*

It could be said that an anticipative weak signal is a *trigger* for the desire or need to make a strategic decision.

VERBATIM 1.4.– (medical equipment sector)

"Our branch in Detroit (USA) read in the newspaper [...] Is this a ruse or an actual *alert* to be taken seriously? Might it be verifiable? Is it likely in view of other information that can be obtained? What other information can we compare this information to?"

"We now need to discover which university laboratory is behind this company. This is one *avenue for investigation*."

"Now we can see clearly that this is *something important…*"

A weak signal may *help discover*, say, the emergence of a new competitor of whom we were not aware, a research project which may yield a new process or a *disruptive technology*, legislation being prepared in a foreign country in which our organization has a presence or where we plan to intervene, etc.

1.4. Weak signals and anticipative strategic scanning

We now turn our attention to what devices are capable of detecting, selecting, storing and interpreting weak signals.

1.4.1. *Anticipative strategic scanning and weak-signal detection*

Weak-signal detection is generally the result of an organizational *process* supported by an information system specifically devoted to strategic management. Such a process is called "strategic scanning" or "anticipative strategic scanning". The expressions "environmental scanning" and "early warning system" are also often used. "An *early warning system* is then a network of actors, practices, resources and technologies that has the common goal of *detecting* and *warning* about an imminent threat so that preventive measures can be taken to control the threat or mitigate its harmful effects" [CHO 09, p. 1072].

Reference	Definition
Hambrick [HAM 81]	"Environmental scanning, the managerial activity of learning about events and trends in the organization's environment, is one of the tasks comprising the broader boundary spanning role. Moreover, environmental scanning can be conceived of as the first step in the ongoing chain of perceptions and actions leading to an organization's adaptation to its environment" [p. 299].
Stoffels [STO 82]	"Environmental scanning as a methodology for coping with issues from outside the firm that may be difficult to observe or diagnose but which cannot be ignored" [p. 7].
Walters *et al.* [WAL 03]	"Environmental scanning is an essential activity undertaken by top executives in order to be effective in steering the organization in a changing environment" [p. 488].
Albright [ALB 04]	"In essence, environmental scanning is a *method* for identifying, collecting and translating information about external influences into useful plans and decisions [...] Environmental scanning – the internal communication of external information about issues that may influence an organization's decision-making process – can identify emerging issues, situations and potential pitfalls that may affect an organization's future" [p. 40].
Kuosa [KUO 10]	"Environmental scanning describes a process where the operational environment of an organisation is systematically scanned for relevant information. The purpose is to identify the early signals of positive environmental change and to detect environmental change already underway" [p. 44].
Lesca *et al.* [LES 12]	"Scanning the environment looking for signs of potential evolution and changes present difficulties" [p. 127]. "Scanning (or *general browsing of data*) is a sort of pre-attentive monitoring or exploration without any particular decision to take or question being identified to guide the research" [p. 132].

Table 1.4. *Definitions of environmental scanning*

The steps in the process are illustrated in Figure 1.6:

1) indication by the hierarchy of an issue which may give rise to a strategic decision later on;

2) definition (or "targeting") of the relevant environment needing to be scanned: building the *"target"*;

3) detection (or retrieval) of the information desired by the managers ("full texts" in the case of textual or digital information);

4) selection of the strictly useful fragments of relevant information (called "briefs");

5) storage of those briefs in the database;

6) interpretation of fragments of information likely to constitute weak signals;

7) diffusion of the weak signals, and the interpretations thereof, to the executives concerned.

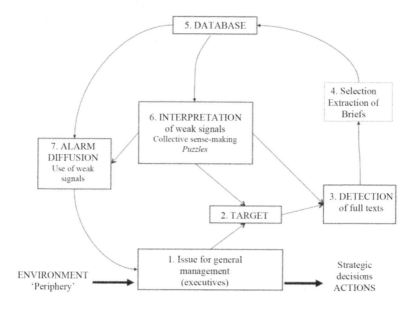

Figure 1.6. *Generic model of the process of anticipative strategic scanning*

Depending on the practices in force within the organization, the process of anticipative strategic scanning is also a process of *organizational learning*, or *knowledge creation*: ideally, it will be continually improved in light of the lessons drawn from experience. "To the extent that an organization's ability to adapt to its outside environment is dependent on knowing and interpreting the external changes that are taking place, *environmental scanning constitutes a primary mode of organizational learning* [...]. Coupled with the availability of information on external change, scanning can induce strategic, generative organizational learning" [CHO 01a, p. 1].

Certain authors distinguish a number of means of *information retrieval* relating to changes of/in the environment. For example:

– "Focused search" versus "Scanning" [VAN 97]. "Focused Search takes place when managers are already involved in a decision-making process, and look for information to better understand the decision context, choices and implications. First a situation that must be decided on is identified, questions are raised and asked, and then a Focused Search is engaged. The objective is to find and gather reliable and non-ambiguous information to give as precise and clear answers as possible to the questions managers wonder. Thus, information evaluation is both analytic and deductive. On the other hand, Scanning is a sort of pre-attentive monitoring or exploration without any particular decision to make or question being identified to guide the research. The objective is to be vigilant to discrepant signs/signals that might manifest in the peripheral vision and could eventually help identify, discover or anticipate plausible changes in the environment. Thus, information evaluation is both heuristic and inductive" [LES 12, pp. 132–133].

– "Conditioned viewing" versus "Undirected viewing". "In undirected viewing, the manager is exposed to information with no specific purpose or information need in mind. In fact, the manager is unaware of what issues might be raised. Undirected viewing takes place all the time, and alerts the manager that 'something' has happened and that there is more to be learned [...] In conditioned viewing, the manager is exposed to information about selected areas or certain types of information. Furthermore, the manager is ready to assess the significance of such information as it is encountered" [CHO 01a, pp. 72–73].

– "Formal search" versus "Informal search". In informal search, the manager actively looks for information to address a specific issue. It is information in that it involves a relatively limited and unstructured effort [...] in formal search, the manager makes a deliberate or planned effort to obtain specific information or information about a specific issue" [CHO 01a, p. 73].

– "Enacting takes place when the organization perceives the environment to be *unanalyzable*. Information needs are those required for experimentation and testing the Environment" [CHO 01b, p. 6/11].

In their own individual ways, these means of information retrieval and of knowing the environment actively contribute to organizational learning.

Such a *process*, because of the instability, or turbulence, of the environment, must constantly take place in light of information gleaned from the ship's radar. "Strategic decision-making by executives in conditions of turbulence are heavily based on continuous environmental scanning for relevant information signals. Furthermore, the continuous acquisition and interpretation of strategic information is critically important to both early warning about discontinuities and better understanding of strategic threats and opportunities" [WAL 92, p. 47].

The operation of the process of "anticipative strategic scanning" is carried out by an *ad hoc* device generally known as a "strategic scanning system", or sometimes a "vigilance system". *"Vigilant information system* (VIS), where vigilance refers to the ability of an information system to help the executive remain alertly watchful for weak signals and discontinuities in the organizational environment symptomatic of emerging strategic threats and opportunities" [WAL 92, p. 37]. "Vigilance denotes the ability of an *information system* to help an executive remain alertly watchful for weak signals and discontinuities in the organizational environment relevant to emerging strategic threats and opportunities" [WAL 92, p. 36].

1.4.2. *The use of weak signals depends on managers' wishes*

In the final analysis, the use of a weak signal depends on the wishes of the organization's executives. *"An early warning system* is then a network of actors, practices, resources, and technologies that has the common goal of *detecting* and *warning* about an imminent threat so that preventive measures can be taken to control the threat or mitigate its harmful effects" [CHO 09, p. 1072]. Another point is whether the signals are actually taken into account by the executives. "This decision is made difficult because the information available is always *ambiguous*, where cues that are true indicators of a threat being present (signal) are intermingled with cues that are generated by chance (noise)" [CHO 09, p. 1076].

In fact, the executives may be interested in weak signals when they are concerned by one of the following two questions:

– Are there weak signals available which relate to the issue at hand? The issue is the trigger and the weak signal is the consequence.

– On which topic might we wonder whether there are weak signals available? The weak signal is the trigger and the executives' wonderings are the consequence.

Such wonderings may make sense when the executives are in search of a new potential strategy for the organization.

1.5. Organizational issues in anticipative strategic scanning, which could weaken strategic decision-making

VERBATIM 1.5.– (various sectors)

"We have a strategic plan covering several years to come. What we need is a device *to help us see* ruptures in the environment coming early enough."

"We do not have any sort of organized system with regard to anticipative environmental scanning. Certainly, pieces of information are given by one person or another, but without a specific goal, on a case-by-case basis, depending on each individual's perception of matters."

"There is information which would help us to anticipate and therefore prepare ourselves, but we do not know where to find that information."

"We go with the flow of events. We do not get ahead of them."

Weak signals are relatively rare: this relative rarity, in conjunction with their characteristics (see Table 1.2), explains why it is natural to expect difficulties when we wish to detect a weak signal. Once the scanning process is begun, the difficulties depend on the chosen target (see Figure 1.7).

Three scenarios may be encountered in practice:

– the target is overly restrictive: we do not look in the right place;

– the target is overly broad: we are overwhelmed with raw data;

– the criteria used to detect a weak signal are not appropriate.

Before examining these three scenarios, let us first narrow down our definition of "targeting" in anticipative strategic scanning.

1.5.1. *Definition of "targeting" of anticipative strategic scanning*

"Targeting" is the operation of building the target on which the weak-signal detection operation will focus. The target is that part of the external environment to which the executives in the organization deem it relevant to focus their attention as a matter of priority, and for a given period. Such is the case, notably, when the executives ask themselves the question: "are there weak signals available which relate to the issue at hand, which would help us to anticipate?"

EXAMPLE 1.9.– (AXA Insurance)

"Our strategy is to invest, on the one hand, in one-off and *targeted* operations to supplement our device – particularly in Asia and Latin America, and on the other hand, in the digitization of the group, which is crucial in order to be able to satisfy customers' expectations" [BER 13].

The target is made up of the names of *topics* and types of *actors* in the organization's relevant environment (see Figure 1.7) [LOZ 13]:

– "An actor is a natural or legal person, external (sometimes internal) to the organization; whose decisions and actions could have an influence on the future of the organization or on activities for which it is responsible. Thus actors to scan are not limited to competitors as suggested in [GIL 03]. They are closer to the notion of stakeholders [FRE 84]."

– A topic is a center of interest when considering the future of the organization" [FRE 84, p. 2].

Actors

	Actor 1	Actor 2	...	Actor N
Topic 1	X			X
Topic 2		X	X	
...	X			
Topic N				X

X denotes a chosen A×T pair

Figure 1.7. *Stub of a target grid*

Examples of types of actor: current or potential competitors, current or prospective customers, current or prospective suppliers and current or prospective partners, etc. The typology therefore needs to be adapted to the executives' interests. Targeting also helps to identify which information *sources* it would be opportune to consult. The target needs to be changeable, because the executives are not able to precisely pinpoint which weak signals they are interested in: by definition, those weak signals are erratic. Thus, the specification of the actors, topics and sources has to be a process of successive approximations. We begin with the few sources we believe to be relevant and then, as the process continues, learn progressively.

VERBATIM 1.6.– (mechanical industry)

"Let us only focus on the important actors. We do not need to add too many. To begin with, we only need to choose a few. We can add more as time goes on..."

"This collective work of building the target represents an opportunity to compare and combine our partial views of the environment... and thereby obtain a fuller picture..."

"This is something we have never done before... it is a little worrying."

The building of the target, depending on how it is done, can have the following consequences.

1.5.2. Insufficient information: too restrictive a target, and the consequences for strategic decision-making

1.5.2.1. Too restrictive a target, too narrow a search field

This case may be encountered in the following situation: the *hierarchy* presents their "strategic vision", and asks the trackers to pick up possible relevant weak signals that may appear within that field of vision... and only within that field of vision.

VERBATIM 1.7.– (R&D, automobile sector)

"At the moment we are thinking only in terms of 'automobiles', but should we not *expand* our field of vision; should our thinking not also relate to the world of the 'stationary'...?"

"We are discovering that there are things we do not know: that there are things which *escape our notice*... which means that we need to *extend* the scope of our scanning to include..."

"Looking at this information, I feel the need to have a *view from a more elevated standpoint*. We ought to be looking at a somewhat *broader* context, because there are pieces of information we are likely to miss."

EXAMPLE 1.10.– (where the hierarchy' strategy relates to innovation in terms of products) [ROH 11]

"In the *strategist role*, corporate foresight directs innovation activities by *creating* a vision, providing strategic guidance, consolidating opinions, assessing and repositioning innovation portfolios, and identifying the new business models of competitors.

– In the *initiator role*, corporate foresight *triggers innovation* initiatives by *identifying new* customer needs, *technologies* and product concepts of competitors.

– In the *opponent role*, corporate foresight challenges the innovators to create better and more successful innovations by challenging basic assumptions, challenging the state-of-the-art of current R&D projects, and scanning for disruptions that could endanger current and future innovations" [ROH 11, p. 237].

1.5.2.2. *Overly restricted peripheral vision, blinkers and blindspot*

Too restrictive a definition of the target brings with it the concepts of "peripheral vision" and "blindspots" [DAY 04]. "Mastering the art of *peripheral vision* is essential to succeeding in a world of *high uncertainty*, even if it is difficult to explore the darker shadows [...] In a fast-moving environment, ask a manager, *what do you pay attention to?*

How do you become better at paying attention to the right things in the periphery without distracting yourself too much from the task at hand? What is the optimal allocation of attention at a given point in time as well as over time? Our focal area can create blindspots: normally, we strike a decent balance between the area of focus and the periphery where we know that blindspots may occur. But what happens when the environment changes so much that the blindspots become danger areas?" [DAY 04, p. 119].

VERBATIM 1.8.– (automobile sector)

"I think we need to re-formalize the picture of the 'target' presented previously, and adapt it *incrementally* to take account of updates... and then work in terms of *differentials*... bring that picture to life... in order to detect the moment when we reach a more critical point."

From an operational viewpoint, the concept of *peripheral vision* does not appear to provide us with a practical response in terms of how to adjust the target. Indeed, how are we to implement the proposed concept? Which methods or working systems should be used? A possible solution will be presented in Chapter 3 of this book (see section 3.1 on TargetBuilder).

1.5.3. *Too much information: consequences of information overload for strategic decision-making*

Such consequences arise when the target is built in an "overzealous" manner, including an excessive number of topics and/or actors.

VERBATIM 1.9.– (automobile sector)

"In hindsight, I think it was a mistake to start with so broad a target. We should have structured things more fully:

what is it that we need? Ask ourselves what we need to focus on to find information faster. Spend a couple of collective brainstorming sessions to target better and determine a clearer red line."

Certain authors write that detecting weak signals requires a 360° scan of the environment. "The turbulent environment requires companies to conduct 360° scans of their environment and prepare for an uncertain future, searching forms and methods to anticipate it" [BAT 11, p. 1031]. The fact is that such authors likely do not have much practical experience, for reasons which will now become apparent.

1.5.3.1. *Definition of "information overload"*

The definitions given by previous authors for "information overload" are many and varied, as shown in Table 1.5.

Put simply, information overload occurs when a person receives far more information than he/she is able to process.

Two pieces of information may appear different because they are presented in different ways, but may actually be identical in terms of content.

"In ordinary language, the term information overload is often used to convey the simple notion of receiving too much information [...]. Within the research community, this everyday use of the term has led to various synonyms, and related terms, such as cognitive overload, sensory overload, communication overload and knowledge overload information which brings out the fatigue syndrome" [LI 11, p. 49]. These authors add that the intensive use of the Internet and other data access techniques will only exacerbate the problem of information overload.

For our purposes here, we will use the definition given by Bettis-Outland [BET 12], shown in the bottom row in

Table 1.5. Our choice is based on the fact that action research conducted in organizations has led us to the following conclusion: ambiguity increases difficulty in detecting and interpreting possible weak signals. Ambiguity leads to the collection of data that only appear different.

Reference	Definition
Nelson [NEL 94]	"Information overload is the *inability to extract* needed knowledge from an immense quantity of information for one of many reasons"[p. 2].
Maltz & Kohli [MAL 96]	"Information overload occurs when new information is transmitted at a rate that exceeds a receiver's capacity to process it" [p. 49].
Bawden *et al.* [BAW 99]	"Information overload occurs when information received becomes a hindrance rather than a help when the information is potentially useful" [p. 249].
Edmunds & Morris [EDM 00]	"However the term is defined, there cannot be many people who have not experienced the feeling of having too much information which uses up too much of their time, causing them to feel stressed which, in turn, affects their decision-making" [p. 19].
Li & Li [LI 11]	*"Information overload* [...] refers to the difficulty a person can have understanding an issue and making decisions that can be caused by the presence of *too much information*. More recently, the topic has been linked with the rapid development of the *Internet usage* and the information explosion in the amount of data" [p. 49].
Bettis-Outland [BET 12]	Information overload is "a multidimensional construct, consisting of three components: (1) equivocality, (2) *quantity* and (3) variety. Equivocality refers to the existence of multiple valid interpretations of information [...]. Quantity measures the *volume* and availability of information, while variety measures the different sources of information. Equivocality refers to the existence of multiple valid interpretations of information" [p. 818].

Table 1.5. *Definitions for "information overload"*

1.5.3.2. *Consequences of information overload for strategic decision-making*

Information overload has numerous undesirable consequences:

– It exacerbates *decision-makers' fatigue*, and it may negatively impact on the quality of the decisions they make. "Information overload, analysis paralysis [...] are all terms currently used to describe the situation when a person is feeling overwhelmed by the quantity of information they have to deal with at work [...] Too much information for the brain to digest leading to an inability to appraise the situation which in turn leads to feelings of extreme weariness. Consequently, the organisation, is likely to suffer from poor decision making or mistakes [...]" [STA 97, p. 2].

– It increases the level of *difficulty in detecting* the relevant information fragments. "Information overload occurs when information received becomes a hindrance, rather than a help when the information is potentially useful" [BET 12, p. 814]. "There are several reasons why environmental scanning may not be effective in an organization. The sheer volume of information may be overwhelming, resulting in an information overload in which important pieces of information may be overlooked or missed" [ALB 04, p. 44].

– It causes *cognitive overload* and decreases attention. The fragmentation of information, the dispersion of the useful fragments and the possibly very high number of them lead to the person's attention being spread too thinly.

VERBATIM 1.10.– (French Ministry of the Economy)

"Everyone is burdened by a mass of fragmentary data which, when viewed separately, are of little interest. It is the combination of those data fragments, and the interpretation we make of them, which is important…"

– It increases the *difficulty of grouping together* the relevant fragments of information, which could enrich one another. "Information overload refers to the difficulty a person can have understanding an issue and making decisions that can be caused by the presence of too much information [...] More recently, the topic has been linked with the rapid development of the Internet usage and the information explosion in the amount of data" [LI 11, p. 49].

– It increases the *difficulty of creating links* between the different fragments of information. "For all the benefits of the information technology and communications revolution, it has a well-known dark side: information overload and its close cousin, attention fragmentation" [DER 11, p. 80]. "Another eerily familiar, if rarely articulated, consequence of information overload is receiving attention from researchers: the *delay in decision making* when you don't know whether or when someone will answer an e-mail message" [HEM 09, p. 85].

VERBATIM 1.11.– (electrical energy industry)

"Things being as they are, we have more and more information available to us. We have to filter and sort through these pieces of information. We are not yet able to sort these information fragments effectively... it is difficult."

"Maybe we do have weak signals available to us. But I have no idea where to look for them."

"The texts we receive cannot be immediately exploited. They are too long. If they do contain the occasional weak signal, those signals are swamped by the rest of the information."

– Finally, information overload could ultimately lead to the demise of an organization: "death by information overload" [HEM 09, p. 83].

1.5.3.3. *Causes of information overload*

One of the causes of information overload may lie in the building of the scanning target. That target may be too broad and not very relevant. Another cause may relate to the inflexibility of the target. In this case, it is practically impossible to change it and adjust it on the basis of experience gained.

1.5.3.3.1. Too wide a target (too broad a search field)

VERBATIM 1.12.–

"Perhaps we shouldn't have started with such a broad target, but spent a couple of sessions targeting the relevant environment better and determining a clearer red line."

"In hindsight, I think it was a mistake to start with so broad a target. We should have structured things more fully: what is it that we need? Ask ourselves what we need to focus on to find information faster."

Given its characteristics, a weak signal does not appear where we want it to, or when we want it to, particularly when the weak signal detection is performed in warning mode (*Scanning or Undirected viewing*).

Consequently, the detection of weak signals would appear to require a constant "360°" scan of the whole of the organization's environment.

In practice, this requirement of 360° vigilance is impossible to satisfy – particularly for reasons of time, cost and expertise.

One solution is to begin by "local scanning" and then *adjusting the target* as more is learnt in how to search for weak signals.

1.5.3.3.2. A moving target

Thus, we can easily see that it is preferable for the scanning target to be moving rather than set in stone. The adjustment can be made on the basis of the weak signals detected and selected previously (see Figure 1.7).

The approach is as follows:

1) A number of topics are chosen, based on a particular issue highlighted by the hierarchy.

2) An information search is launched.

3) The results thus obtained reveal one or more actors.

VERBATIM 1.13.– (medical equipment industry)

"We now need to *discover* which *university* laboratory is behind this start-up. This is one avenue for investigation."

The target is enriched with the names of those actors. This enrichment may only be momentary.

The first stub of the target is thus built.

4) A search for information about those actors will provide further information about the actors themselves and about their areas of activity.

5) This new information will likely enable us to refine our initial topics, and to discover connected topics of which we were not aware or did not know enough about, etc.

Figure 1.8 illustrates the dynamics of the target's evolution. This evolution will continue until the search area is sufficiently refined to produce the desired weak signals.

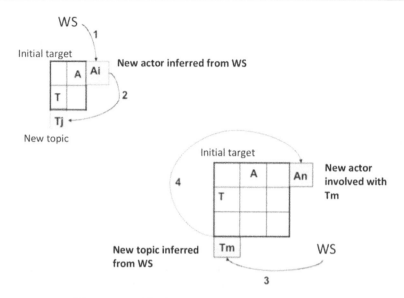

Figure 1.8. *Weak signal versus target evolution*

1.5.4. *Detecting a weak signal in an information-overload situation (in a full text)*

1.5.4.1. *Difficulties in distinguishing a zoom in/zoom out weak signal*

The difficulty in discerning a possible weak signal may arise from the fact that it is contained within too general, or indeed too detailed, a text. What trackers need, if possible, is a sort of magnifying glass which would enable them to "zoom in" on a specific piece of data to distinguish relevant details about it, or indeed an instrument to zoom out and obtain a less myopic, and more meaningful, overall view.

Moss Kanter suggests [MOS 11] that "leaders need multiple perspectives to get a complete picture. Effective leaders zoom in and zoom out [...] *Zoom in*, and get a close look at select details – perhaps too close to make sense of them [...] *Zoom out,* and see the big picture – but perhaps miss some subtleties and nuances [...] Zooming out is appropriate for top leaders [...] They can *zoom in* to see problems while zooming *out* to look for similar situations" [MOS 11, p. 112]

How, though, do we zoom in and out?

– *Zoom in*: evidently, this operation involves taking a closer look at a fragment of text contained in a more substantial information source, e.g. a text of hundred lines. It is therefore necessary to have software which enables us to examine a small fragment of information. The software then acts as a magnifying glass.

– *Zoom out*: this operation is precisely the opposite: beginning with a small fragment of information, we view it in a broader context, in much the same way as a telescope can be used to observe a star in a *constellation* or in a galaxy. Alternatively, we can combine that fragment of information with other elements that can add to it. This operation should enable us to better understand the information fragment, to overcome any ambiguity, reduce misunderstandings, identify any contradictions, and confirm our interpretation of it.

Viewed in this light, *zoom in* and *zoom out* operations are very useful, particularly in an information-overload situation, either to look closely at a particular information fragment or to combine an information fragment with other fragments within a larger whole, lending it more meaning. Yet the authors of previous works in the field do not specify how these operations could be performed. They make no mention of any available systems. We will put forward a suggestion in Chapter 3.

1.5.4.2. *Characteristics used to distinguish a weak signal*

What are the characteristic traits that can help recognize a possible weak signal when it is isolated? When given a piece of data, how can we recognize that it may yield a weak signal? What are the characteristic signs to base our thinking on?

VERBATIM 1.14.– (agro-food industry)

"What exactly is a 'weak signal'? I understand what it is in theory, and what I'm asking here is not a question of definition, but rather a very concrete question. China's international academic publications (in our sector) have massively increased over the past few months. What sort of information does that give me? In particular, how do I pick out any weak signals that are there? If I'm honest, it's a little bit beyond me."

VERBATIM 1.15.– (chemical sector)

"I would like to know how to distinguish a weak signal within a huge mass of irrelevant data."

1.5.4.3. *Dispersed versus grouped information fragments*

VERBATIM 1.16.– (energy industry: head of sales)

"With regard to potential customers, the information that we have is extremely *fragmented* and *dispersed*. Each piece of information means very little when viewed *in isolation*."

"We are not used to *pooling our information*, and reflect all together about what all this information could mean in terms of a competitor or a major client."

1.6. Conclusion: concepts discussed, issues noted and resulting requirements

The concepts relating to anticipative strategic scanning to aid in strategic decision-making suggested by previous authors are rather numerous. However, their application in organizations is, as yet, problematic, as attested by the verbatim quotes given throughout this book.

VERBATIM 1.17.– (agro-food industry)

"We try to take more of a pro-active approach, to anticipate the needs of the group's divisions before they arise... but it's not easy. Certainly we have feelers out, we search in every possible direction, we sort, *we cross-reference* and try to shed light on potential areas for development. We need to find *snippets of information* about subjects which we don't know whether or not will be of interest, to work in that nebulous, fuzzy environment... to detect potential possibilities. At present, *we do not yet have a sufficiently proactive approach*, and *less still the appropriate systems.*"

Of the various concepts put forward in previous literature on the subject, two appear to be particularly relevant in terms of the issue of weak signals: "Peripheral vision" and "Blindspot":

– if the weak signal is hidden in a "blindspot", then it is impossible to detect it;

– if it is not possible to compare the weak signal against other pieces of information that could confirm it, add to it or else contradict it, then the weak signal probably loses a lot of its usefulness.

These two concepts raise the question of "How can we...?" This question is also raised by the concept of the "scanning Target": how can we build the target appropriately and adapt it on the basis of weak signals previously collected.

The difficulties in implementing the concepts are twofold:

– the attitude of leaders who are still relatively voluntaristic in regard to anticipative strategic scanning, on the one hand;

– the perceived inaptitude of computer-based systems appropriate for exploitation of the weak signals gathered by anticipative strategic scanning, on the other hand.

In Chapter 2, we present the responses proposed by various authors in the existing literature.

State of the Art: Systems Suggested by Previous Authors

Entry point and line of argument: as we did in section 1.2, in this chapter, we again begin our discussion at the end of the process of anticipative strategic scanning, i.e. interpreting weak signals and making sense of them to detect the obstacles needed to be overcome before arriving at this final stage. We will then work backwards, step-by-step, eventually coming to the beginning of the process, i.e. the detection of briefs (possible weak signals), in order to target the scanning effectively. It should be noted that this approach is taken on the basis of the needs expressed by the organizations with which we conducted our action research

VERBATIM 2.1.– (French Ministry of the Economy)

"The Puzzle method for interpreting weak signals and collectively making sense is very interesting. However, I find myself wondering what to do in order to prepare the briefs used. One has to go looking for them in enormous quantities of raw data. Without a system to automate that task, it is not possible to exploit weak signals, in view of a lack of time... and of the cost of the work needing to be done!"

In other words, the question of interpretation of the briefs (possible weak signals) does not even arise unless that input has previously been obtained. The question is whether computer systems are available to carry out these operations in the context of information overload. Thus, let us begin with the operation "Interpretation of possible weak signals/collective sense-making": what does this operation require?

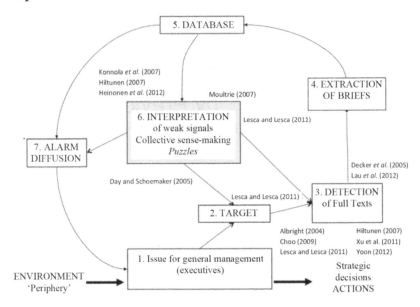

Figure 2.1. *Position of systems proposed by previous authors relative to the generic model*

Figure 2.1 shows the name of the authors in the position in the process of anticipative strategic scanning corresponding to their contribution.

2.1. Entry point: collective interpretation of a set of homogeneous weak signals to make sense

The process of interpreting weak signals is difficult to formalize, and more so to model. "The strategic management and organizational decision-making literature agree that both strategic issue identification and strategic decision-making are *ill-structured processes* and neither is well understood" [WAL 92, p. 42]. It is the preserve of human beings, because it involves imagination and creativity: "analyzing weak signals requires individuals to imagine how weak signals could evolve in the future and how they can impact other developments or be linked to new or existing products or services. Thus, creativity, openness... are central in the search of weak signals [SCH 13b, p. 2]. Interpreting multiple weak signals together means that we seek to create connections between them: "sense-making itself is concerned with the creation of meaningful connections through the combination of extracted cues with frames of reference in order to enable interpretation and sense attribution" [SCH 13b, p. 3]. However, in practice, there are systems that can aid in the interpretation process.

What systems are proposed by the existing literature to help interpret any possible weak signals?

VERBATIM 2.2.– (energy industry: head of sales)

"With regard to potential customers, the information that we have is extremely *fragmented* and *dispersed*. Each piece of information means very little when viewed *in isolation*."

"We are not used to *pooling our information*, and reflect all together about what all this information could mean in terms of a competitor or a major client."

We will present three methods, giving a fuller discussion of the third as it is very often encountered in numerous organizations.

2.1.1. *Interpreting weak signals: sense-making*

Konnola *et al.* put forward the *RPM Screening* method to collectively interpret weak signals with a view to uncovering any innovations [KÖN 07]. The data for interpretation are projected onto a screen for collective viewing. *RPM Screening* offers a support for collective work to help in the construction of a collective vision on a given issue – primarily relating to innovation. One particular point is that the participants can work as part of a remote network. They do not need to travel to meet in the same place. "We develop a collaborative foresight method RPM Screening (method for the scanning of weak signals) which consists of phases for the distributed generation, mutual commenting, iterative revision, multi-criteria evaluation and portfolio analysis of innovation ideas" [MOS 11, p. 608].

In particular, the *RPM Screening* method is intended toward:

– favoring the *production of innovative ideas* on the basis of the reflections triggered by any possible weak signals (i.e. *innovative ideas as reflections of weak signals*);

– facilitating the proposal by the participants of relations between the weak signals obtained in isolation (*to see how the signals relate to one another*);

– helping the participants to devise mini-scenarios;

– avoiding fragmental decision-making entities.

The implementation of the method involves the following steps:

– "to engage *a larger number of participants* in the theme area work, beyond the some 10–20 named participants who were closely involved in the work of each theme area;

– to develop a systematic *foresight method* for the scanning, elaboration, evaluation and analysis of *weak signals* in view of multiple perspectives;

– to deploy this method in each theme area;

– to disseminate the results to a wider audience" [MOS 11, p. 612].

The first application of the pilot project was carried out by the *Ministry of Trade and Industry in Finland*.

Detection of weak signals	Interpretation of weak signals	Participants in collective work
Not indicated	Human/manual	Multiple separate spaces

Table 2.1. *Recap on RPM Screenings method [KÖN 07]*

2.1.2. *How about sense-making using images, remotely?*

Heinonen *et al.* present a method called *"Futures Window"* [HEI 12]. The goal of the method is to enable the weak signals detected to trigger new ideas in the minds of R&D and Innovation teams. "Where visual weak signals are used to trigger futures thinking and innovation in organisations [...]. The method used by the *Futures* Window is to display weak signals in a visual form as a slide show on a large screen with the aim of encouraging people to anticipate and innovate futures" [HEI 12, p. 248].

In the "Futures Window" method:

– the "Weak signals" are images (*They can be represented as images: photos, paintings, drawings, video clips, etc.*) rather than fragments of text. These are referred to as "visual weak signals";

– these images are *diffused exactly as they are* to potential users, in the hope that:

- they will trigger an idea in the minds of the receivers,

- they will be discussed and interpreted collectively *(the users participate collectively in detecting the visual weak signals)*,

- the collective work is carried out *remotely* using various communication technologies, in particular by *sending multimedia messages* via *mobile phone*.

"The Futures Window could be a central tool to be used in Creative Foresight Spaces (CFS). The concept of CFS is offered as one way of responding to the growing demand for innovation in corporations and work organisations. The FW method was tested at VTT Technical Research Centre" [HEI 12, p. 252].

Detection of weak signals	Interpretation of weak signals	Participants in collective work
Not indicated	Human/manual	Multiple separate spaces

Table 2.2. *Recap on "Futures Window" [HEI 12]*

2.1.3. Puzzle method: example

The team at the CERAG-CNRS laboratory [LES 11] advanced the Puzzle method for collectively interpreting a set of possible weak signals to make sense of them and prepare potential strategic decisions.

We will now briefly present this method, basing ourselves on an example worked on by the Institut National de la Recherche Agronomique (INRA) [National Agronomic Research Institute], France.

The strategic question for the session was this: does the change in arable surface area spell serious problems for China? Might it present an opportunity for INRA to put its skills to good (and profitable) use?

Figure 2.2 shows the result of a Puzzle session. We will now comment on it briefly.

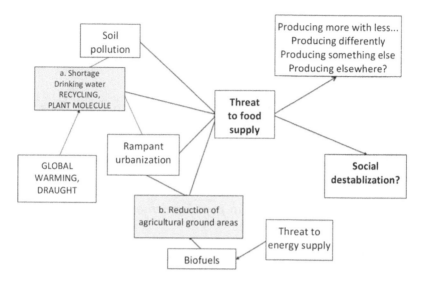

Figure 2.2. *China puzzle devised by INRA*

2.1.3.1. *Discovering briefs*

At the beginning of the session, the animator distributes the file of information (the *full texts*) that he/she has gathered, and the *briefs* he/she has prepared.

EXAMPLE 2.1.– (a few examples of briefs used during the session)

China has less than 9% of arable land on the planet; yet its food production sustains 22% of the world's population.

Drought is affecting the Yangtze Basin (which represents 5% of cultivable land and 3.29 million inhabitants).

The Chinese Premier has declared that China must be stringent in the application of the regulations concerning the protection of *cultivatable land*.

The Chinese Premier has called for more eco-friendly land use: in the face of the *rampant urbanization*, construction advocates must not use arable land for their new projects.

Global warming is worsening from year to year: does the introduction of different food crops need to be envisaged?

There is a marked increase in the number of gasoline-burning vehicles: this poses a *threat to the energy supply*.

There is a notable rise in *popular demonstrations* in many areas, etc.

The full texts have been collected separately by a number of people, in accordance with their respective fields. The participants propose to arrange the briefs on the screen (spatial arrangement disposition) in such a way as to reveal a plausible concatenation of events, and thus make sense of those information fragments (see Figure 2.2).

2.1.3.2. *Method*

The participants comment on each of the briefs in turn. They suggest ways of arranging the briefs on the screen (i.e. their spatial disposition) in a way that illustrates a plausible succession of events, and thus make sense of those information fragments (see Figure 2.2).

Multiple different spatial arrangements are envisaged, one-by-one. The participants argue in support of their own ideas. Reasoned reflections and interpretations emerge, as is illustrated by the quotations below.

The puzzle gradually evolves in light of the exchanges between the participants. A breakdown of this process is given in the literature.

VERBATIM 2.3.– (examples of utterances during a Puzzle session)

1) "This piece of information needs to be in synergy with that other piece of information…"

2) "Looking at this puzzle, it *makes me think that…*"

3) "What you're saying certainly *complements* what's on the screen… that seems to be the *missing link* between the two pieces of information…"

4) "Does that mean that a *decision needs to be taken quickly…?*"

5) "I wouldn't have said this five minutes ago, *but now* I *think that…*"

6) "I think what you just said *can be linked back to* something else that's preying on my mind…"

7) "I'd like to revisit fragment n… I'm wondering *whether anybody has any more detail about this…*"

8) "This discussion has *brought to light a danger* which we might have been under-estimating…"

9) "This fragment forms the link between fragment x and fragment y…"

10) "Usually, everyone analyzes their own information in a *restricted context*; here it is quite the opposite… This collective reflection we are conducting here triggers a sort of resonance in our minds…"

11) "The fact of suggesting *connections* between the different information fragments provides an additional level of interpretation which is of crucial importance in the task of sense-making… it reminds me of the network of connections which are forged in the brain…"

12) "It is important to be able to conduct a dialog on the basis of information like this… it *sheds light on issues* which

I hadn't thought of, which are beyond the scope of my usual concerns..."

13) President of INRA: "We can see that the factors which will influence agriculture are likely to come *primarily from outside* of agriculture... and consequently that we need to engage in strategic scanning with regard to other actors, other approaches...", etc.

2.1.3.3. *Result*

At the end of the session, it has been found that there are several opportunities in China where INRA could bring its skills to bear and obtain major supply contracts. It is still to be determined which strategic decisions this could lead to, on the part of the executives at INRA.

The application of the Puzzle method was repeated a hundred or so times by a wide variety of organizations. The procedure used was agreed upon and accepted by the participants. The method has aroused a great deal of interest, but the following questions have also been raised:

– Regarding the *place* where the participants meet, do they necessarily have to come together in the same physical location?

For the time being, the answer is that they need to be in the same place. However, there has been a situation where the participants met in Sao Paulo (Brazil) and the animator was in Grenoble (France). The animation then took place by way of videoconferencing.

VERBATIM 2.4.–

"Is it absolutely necessary to bring participants together in the same place to make sense using this method? What can we do if the participants are in very distant locations – sometimes in different countries?"

"How were the initial data gathered, and how were the briefs which we used extracted? Is there a system which could help us with this?"

– With regard to the *automation* of puzzles stored in the database, is it possible to keep these puzzles updated automatically?

For the moment, the answer is "no". The Puzzle method does not indicate how to obtain weak signals before collective interpretation sessions. One possible solution, regarding the obtaining of possible weak signals before interpretation of the full texts, has now become available (see section 3.2).

VERBATIM 2.5.–

"It would be helpful if the puzzles could be enriched automatically, as new information becomes available."

"I think it would be useful for the software itself to be able to suggest a certain number of possible puzzles. After that, we, the users, would validate them, correct them, or maybe add new ones."

"You should be able to navigate through the database, from puzzle to puzzle."

– With regard to the workspace where the collective interpretation sessions take place, it seems feasible to draw on the suggestion put forward by Moultrie *et al.* [MOU 07]: "workspaces to create desirable spatial interactions [...] dedicated spaces to support group creativity and encourage creativity [...] physical environment in supporting creativity and innovation is sparse and somewhat fragmented" [MOU 07, p. 53].

Detection of weak signals	Interpretation of weak signals	Participants in collective work
Not indicated	Human/manual + formalized procedure supplied	Single space

Table 2.3. *Recap of the Puzzle method [LES 11]*

2.2. Directly detecting a weak signal in a full text

VERBATIM 2.6.– (examples drawn from visits to organizations)

"Maybe we do have weak signals available to us. But I have no idea where to look for them."

"We have a strategic plan covering several years to come. What we need is a device *to help us see* ruptures in the environment coming early enough."

"The texts we receive cannot be immediately exploited. They are too long. If they do contain the occasional weak signal, those signals are swamped by the rest of the information."

"Things being as they are, we have more and more information available to us. We have to sort through these pieces of information. We are not yet able to sort these information fragments effectively... it is difficult."

Generally speaking, managers want to have direct access to the weak signals as such, in a form that is immediately useful for them in making their decisions: particularly when those signals represent early warnings indicating that x or y decision needs to be taken. "This method allows managers to get only that information that they determine is necessary for making decisions, to ask questions, and to control the flow of information, which is not possible when depending on a book or report" [ALB 04, p. 43].

Yet it is difficult to directly detect a "ready-to-use" weak signal, particularly when it is swamped in a big mass of data, creating noise. "The sheer volume of information may be overwhelming, resulting in an information overload in which important *pieces of information* may be overlooked or missed" [MOU 07, p. 44].

Often, the executives are not keen to pay attention to a weak signal, for fear of false alarms. This observation led Choo to conduct an in-depth study on the "construction of risk" [CHO 09]: "We contextualize these issues in a broader discussion of the social construction of risk and its consequences on policy and risk management" [CHO 09, p. 1071].

RECAP.– It has not been possible to identify any publication putting forward an aid for operational detection (automated or manual) of weak signals.

There is still no substitute for human discernment. This, in turn, requires appropriate training of the human agents, the "trackers" of weak signals.

A few past authors have put forward systems to train human agents in weak-signal detection [BLA 03, ILM 06, LES 11].

2.3. Automatically selecting a "useful" information fragment (a "brief", for our purposes)

2.3.1. *Data overload versus "useful" information fragments*

VERBATIM 2.7.– (examples drawn from visits to organizations in the industrial sector)

"We have a huge *volume* of information, in all sorts of forms: electronic messages, reviews, etc."

"99% of everything published in not relevant for the automobile industry; 1% is relevant."

"I don't want another series of summaries passed along the hierarchical chain. I want the relevant information, in usable form."

"The information needs to be *brief*: 2–3 lines per fragment... I'm not looking for a thesis."

"Rather than having complete information, but too late, it would be better to have only *one line* of information indicating where I can find the complete text."

"We are not able to automatically thresh out the useful information. We do that as and when required, on a daily basis."

Human detection of briefs likely to contain a weak signal raises an almost prohibitive difficulty, because of the increase in the volumes of *full texts* obtained by systematic use of the Internet – in particular for data mining.

Hiltunen carried out a survey, put to experts in charge of environmental scanning for organizations [HIL 07]. The question related to the importance they attach to the information sources they habitually use to discover weak signals. Even in 2007, the Internet was already playing a very important part (with Internet resources, online databases, etc.). Today, that importance has considerably increased.

The necessity for automated systems to help select the fragments of information likely to contain weak signals is becoming increasingly apparent. "Hence it is imperative to develop a comprehensive framework for web-based weak signal detection which covers the following three steps:

– Searching and filtering (i.e. the web in the present case) pieces or fragments of information containing relevant hints at future developments.

– Collecting and storing these information fragments in a way that ensures transparency of historical developments.

– Assembling the meanings of various information fragments to conclude the weak signals.

To put this into practice requires recourse to the contextual environment" [DEC 05, p. 193].

However, does this research, which is often very academic in nature, actually correspond to the needs felt in organizations?

2.3.2. *Managers want automation of information detection*

Xu *et al.* set out to discover whether managers wished the whole of the process of anticipative strategic scanning to be automated (by a system for information scanning, filtering, interpretation and alerting) [XU 11]. To that end, they performed a survey in large organizations. They targeted their questions with a view to evaluate the following hypotheses:

– "H1. Executives perceive an intelligent information scanning agent to be highly useful to acquire strategic information.

– H2. Executives perceive an information filtering agent highly useful to reduce information overload and to increase information relevancy.

– H3. Executives perceive an information interpretation agent highly useful to make sense of information.

– H4. Executives perceive an intelligent agent sending vigilant alerts highly useful to keep them informed wherever they are." [XU 11, p. 190]

The results obtained are as follows:

– H1. Detection: managers are already extremely busy, and they would like the tasks relating to anticipative strategic scanning to be automated as far as possible (*i.e. they want a system for information scanning, filtering, interpretation and alerting*), but with significant differences depending on the task at hand. Data collection must be automated.

– H2. Filtering: the filtering of the data to select the useful information fragments ought to be automated.

– H3. Interpretation: the interpretation of the information selected, and sense-making, must not be automated. *Interpretation of the information is, and must remain, the managers' job.*

– H4. Diffusion: the alerting of the executives concerned by the information should be automated. It is vital that they be able to make their decisions as quickly as possible.

These survey results vindicate research efforts aimed at automating the detection of useful information within big volumes of raw data and limiting data overload. In the third part of this book, we will put forward one solution: APROXIMA).

In addition to the above results, the following two points should be borne in mind:

– We must distinguish between "data overload", which refers to an excess of raw data, and "information overload", which could refer to an excess of potentially useful information, without specifying the recipient to whom each fragment of information could be useful. If all managers receive all of the information that is "useful to someone", this is certainly information overload.

– It is also essential to distinguish between "potentially useful information" and a "weak signal". Any "weak signal" should, in theory, be useful, as it has been interpreted as such. Yet not all potentially useful information is necessarily a weak signal, which will help in anticipating the future. It could be a strong signal, or simply useful for the day-to-day management of the organization.

2.3.3. *Is it possible to automate the detection of potentially useful information?*

The answer is "yes", according to Decker *et al.'s* [DEC 05]'s experiment. Decker took the following question as a starting point: is it realistic to think that an appropriate system could be as effective as a human agent in detecting relevant full texts (in relation to a given issue) within a big corpus of raw data? He performed an experiment corresponding to what might happen in an organization. Our presentation of his experiment is given below.

Experiment: use of the *environmental scanning system* (system).

The experiment comprises the following steps:

– choice of the area of the environment to be scanned: finance, tips concerning future investments, etc.;

– choice of the information source to be scanned on the Internet: Reuters;

– choice of a period of time during which the *full texts* must have been published;

– first, a group of words (called "information fragments") is provided by an expert in the domain. That group of words will be used to search for texts likely to be of interest.

Text mining on the Reuters database produced 50 full texts. Now, from those 50 texts, we need to select only the relevant texts. Here is where the true experiment begins. It consists of detecting relevant *full texts* in two different ways. In both cases, the time allotted for the detection is 12 min, in order to simulate the time pressure imposed by the hierarchical superiors in the organization. Thus, only a truly superficial selection is performed, with a view to preserving realism in the experiment.

The selection is performed twice: once by a human being and once by the prototype environmental scanning system, and the two results obtained are compared:

– Human selection of texts from the 50 full texts. The expert needs to read the texts within the bounds of the time allotted for the task. Practically speaking, in these conditions of information overload, he/she can only cast a superficial eye over the texts, and probably not all of them at that. In the experiment, the expert was able to select only 18 texts that he felt were relevant. The experiment was repeated with 25 people with expertise in the domain in question – assistants to a senior manager.

– Automated selection of texts by the *ES System* prototype, over the course of the 12 min allowed. The software uses the technique known as "Information Foraging Theory" (IFT) to detect the texts, out of the 50 given, which it deems relevant. It should be noted that, previously, 125 different texts from the Reuters database had been used in the training process undergone by the system "Knowledge Infrastructure".

– Comparison of results. All of the texts selected by the expert were among the texts selected automatically. The software had also selected additional texts, which the expert was not able to read, due to lack of time. It then needed to be seen whether the system had "done a good job". Experts read the texts detected by the software and found that the majority (three out of four) of the additional texts selected by the software were indeed relevant.

– The experiment showed that, at least in this case, automated detection of relevant texts within a big corpus of "raw" texts is a wise choice: it helps gain a great deal of time, and limits the danger of leaving out possibly relevant texts.

The issue raised above (in section 2.3.3) by managers in the organizations could, therefore, actually be solved by an automated system. We will return to this topic in Chapter 3.

2.3.4. *Prototype of a device to filter data obtained from Web 2.0: ABIMA*

Lau *et al.* created a prototype for a device to detect and filter data obtained from Web 2.0 [LAU 12]. The device is called *ABIMA* (*Adaptive Business Intelligence for Mergers and Acquisitions*).

An experiment is presented below, relating to decision-making in regard to mergers and/or acquisition of organizations.

Expected output: ABIMA should represent a decision-support system with regard to potential mergers and/or acquisitions. This support comes in the form of information: ABIMA provides *short summaries* that make up a dashboard. The information detected by ABIMA relate to the "sentiment" and comments expressed by investors. These information fragments are extracted from *online messages* harvested from Web 2.0. They express investors' *opinions* regarding change on the *Dow Jones stock index*. "The main research questions addressed by our study are summarized as follows: is the proposed computational method for domain specific sentiment analysis more effective than other existing methods?" [LAU 12, p. 1241]. Such information does already exist on Web 2.0, but it is generally difficult to access. Mining of that information, when performed manually, requires a great deal of time because of *information overload*.

Frequency of data mining: the constant scanning of the specific domain target and analysis of the information found on Web 2.0 produce a result in the form shown in Figure 2.3.

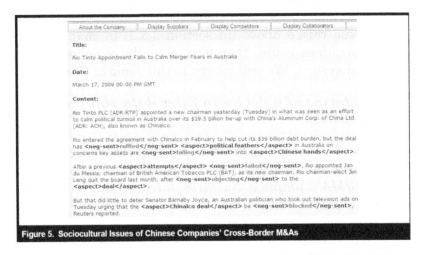

Figure 2.3. *Example of the output produced by ABIMA [LAU 12]*

In the generic process of anticipative strategic scanning (see Figure 1.6), ABIMA relate to the steps of targeting, detection of relevant information fragments and shaping of those information fragments.

Restriction: ABIMA is necessarily limited to a specific domain (specific target), because of the lexicon that it uses. A specialized lexicon relating to the specific domain chosen (Mergers and Acquisitions, in this case) needs to be constructed beforehand.

Learning: ABIMA is adaptive in the sense that the initial lexicon, constructed by human experts, is then enriched as the program learns, while remaining targeted at the domain chosen initially. The lexicon is enriched automatically, using an *ad hoc* algorithm. Hence, ABIMA is capable of being very effective, because it learns the expressions used in the chosen domain. The authors speak of "Adaptive Business Intelligence for Mergers and Acquisitions".

The authors illustrate their explanations with an experiment, relating largely to the organization RIO TINTO.

Experiment: the result of the experiment is a dashboard where, for each industrial section, users can see:

– the most financially stable organizations;

– the organizations best equipped to adapt to sociocultural changes;

– the organizations that have improved their situation by organizational adaptation;

– the most competitive organizations.

The dashboard thus obtained essentially reveals capability information.

The authors do not specify whether their suggestion for weak signal detection relates to Focused search or Conditioned viewing mode, or to Warning mode (also referred to as Scanning or Undirected viewing).

Thus, it seems it is possible to detect/filter the data obtained from *messages* circulating on *Web 2.0* and produce short summaries using the ABIMA prototype. In this case, the summaries relate to the "sentiments" and comments expressed on Web 2.0 in the *target domain*. Thus, scanning is performed *continuously*. However, ABIMA is limited to the domain that was originally targeted. ABIMA's lexicon is adaptive: it is automatically enriched with words relating to the target domain.

2.4. Improving weak-signal detection by improving the target

2.4.1. *What should we scan for in the environment?*

Given its characteristics, a weak signal does not appear where we want it to, or when we want it to, particularly when the weak signal detection is performed in warning mode (*Scanning or Undirected viewing*). Consequently, the detection of weak signals would appear to require a constant "360°" scan of the whole of the organization's environment.

In practice, this requirement of 360° vigilance is impossible to satisfy – particularly for reasons of time and cost.

One solution is to begin by "local scanning" and then adjusting the target as more is learnt in the search for weak signals.

2.4.2. *Learning about the boundary of the environment being scanned*

Another result from Hiltunen's aforementioned study [HIL 07] is as follows: "An important update for these results is mentioned by Day and Shoemaker [DAY 06, pp. 56–59], who underline the periphery as a source of weak signals for the future. Day and Shoemaker emphasize the potentiality of Internet and blogs as good sources for scanning the *periphery*" [DAY 06, p. 12]. This concept was introduced earlier on in our own discussion. It means, in particular, that it may be fruitful to scan beyond the boundary of the target chosen initially.

VERBATIM 2.8.– (chemical industry)

"Is it not wise to think about the whole of the process rather than just that part which directly affects us? If we take the problem of plastic out of its immediate context (its environment), our results become much less significant [...] We need to look at what happens in Russia or in the Ukraine, for example, where they are capable of dealing with it [...]"

(Banking sector) "Where might we find additional information to help enrich the information we have at the moment?"

The authors do not give any practical indications regarding how to implement the concept of "peripheral vision". The foray into the world beyond the initial boundary of the target will likely be by trial and error.

2.4.3. *An automated technique to help change an organization's peripheral vision*

Yoon proposed what might be called a preparatory approach, to be performed in advance of the weak signal detection itself [YOO 12].

Method: the technique offers a way to circumvent the problem of information overload. Yoon designed an automated method. More specifically, this procedure needs to be capable of detecting "weak signal topics". In this case, the proposed procedure appears as a support for the building of the scanning "target" and a way of expanding the organization's field of view. "Therefore, the peripheral vision to detect weak signals is important because it provides business experts with key concepts for identifying business opportunities of alternative futures" [YOO 12, p. 12543].

Method: the automated method uses "text mining" based on the occurrence and co-occurrence of keywords, and on graph analysis.

Definition: "Text mining is different from regular data mining in that the patterns in text mining are obtained by processing natural language text rather than structured databases, by exploiting natural language processing and keyword matching" [YOO 12, p. 12543].

The steps in the procedure are as follows:

– collection of web news using Web news articles, and storage in a database;

– "keyword *extraction*" on the basis of their frequency in the texts;

– removal of irrelevant words;

– *keyword definition*: "defining keywords concerning environmental factors, business needs and product/technological components" [YOO 12, p. 12546];

– construction of *keyword portfolio maps* using text mining;

– the map (also known as a "keyword emergence map" or "keyword issue map" reveals keywords;

– "Identification of weak signal *topics*", "visual/statistical data news search" [YOO 12, p. 12546].

Characteristics of Yoon's method and results obtained:

– the procedure is *quantitative*: "identifying weak signal topics by *statistical analysis*", "The proposed *quantitative procedure* generates...";

– the selection is based on the frequency of the terms in the document;

– the output data are "two types of keyword portfolio *maps*, the keyword emergence *map* and the keyword issue *map*, by using the *occurrence information of keywords* and time-weighted analysis" [YOO 12, p. 12546];

– the scanning is (most likely) iterative.

EXAMPLE 2.2.–

Yoon illustrates his ideas with an example relating to the topic of solar/photovoltaic energy ("using Web news articles related to solar cells") [YOO 12, p. 12546]. In the interests of comparison, the example of the APROXIMA system's application presented later on in this book will also relate to solar cells.

Shortcomings of the method:

– Yoon's automated method *does not produce briefs*. Neither does it appear to use "anticipative" keywords. From these two perspectives, it could be considered to be complementary to the *APROXIMA* system (see section 3.3);

– the author does not specify whether his suggestion is most appropriate for detecting weak signals in conditioned viewing or warning mode (Scanning, or Undirected viewing).

2.5. Conclusion

Table 2.4 gives an overview of the partial conclusions drawn from each of the steps followed in this chapter.

A number of methods and systems have recently been proposed by various authors in the field. In this chapter, we have presented some of the most recent methods. These methods and systems are intended to support strategic decision-making by ensuring an in-depth knowledge of the environment and changes within it. Yet these propositions are only very partial: a great deal of work needs to be done and, as P. Rossel writes, "early detection [is] an *open avenue for research*" [ROS 12, p. 236]. Specifically, the results of new research are presented in Chapter 3. This research is aimed at contributing to the use of weak signals in strategic decision-making.

Name of method	For automated interpretation of weak signals	For human interpretation of weak signals	For automated brief detection	For filtering the data obtained	Aid to evolving targeting
Puzzle Lesca and Lesca [LES 11]	N/A	Procedure and partial software support	N/A	N/A	N/A
RPM Screening Konnola *et al.* [KÖN 07]	N/A	Procedure and software support for remote work	N/A	N/A	N/A
Futures Window Heinonen and Hiltunen [HEI 12]	N/A	No procedure, software support for remote work	N/A	N/A	N/A
ES System Decker *et al.* [DEC 05]	N/A	N/A	Detection of full texts only	N/A	N/A
ABIMA Lau *et al.* [LAU 12]	N/A	N/A	Only capability information	N/A	N/A
Text mining Yoon [YOO 12]	N/A	N/A	Detection of "weak-signal topics"	N/A	N/A

N/A = Not applicable.

Table 2.4. *State of the art regarding the systems designed by the various authors in the field*

3

Proposed Systems: Results of Information System Prototyping Research Conducted at the CNRS-CERAG Lab (France)

The expression "information system prototyping" [BAS 98] denotes a method of experimental *action research*, the response to which involves iterative steps of design and testing of a system as a support for decision-making or performance of a task.

The starting point for the research is often a lack of know-how expressed by an organization (an *in situ* problem in the field). The research is therefore aimed at producing *actionable knowledge*, i.e. an answer to the question "How do we..." which provides an acceptable and practicable solution to the lack of know-how expressed by the organization's managers. The research involves the following steps:

– the design of a solution is first presented in the form of a procedure (P) and then in the form of a prototype for a system;

– the research question is expressed in the form of a hypothesis: "*IF* the system is used in the following conditions, *THEN* the organization should be noticeably better equipped to make the decision (D)";

– the results obtained are "situated" or "one-off" results. To expand their applicability, we need to *repeat the experiment* with other organizations.

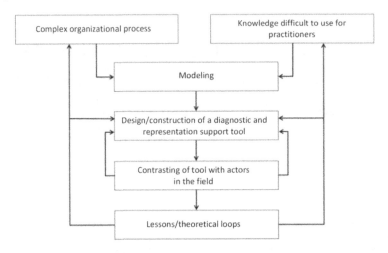

Figure 3.1. *Information system prototyping*

3.1. TARGETBUILDER, an aid to targeting scanning priorities

3.1.1. *Usefulness*

TARGETBUILDER helps users of the Target method [LOZ 13]: it is a support for the collective building of the target for anticipative strategic scanning. The concept of a target was defined previously (section 1.5.1).

TARGETBUILDER is an interactive system used in meeting rooms when managers want to collectively build their scanning target and express their information needs.

It is possible that, *a priori*, the managers will share neither the same interests nor the same vocabulary, and that each of them will have a fragmented and fuzzy understanding of the topics which the organization needs to be scanning. In these instances, *collective* targeting helps reduce these problems, with a consensual representation of the environment being built, and helps clarify the organization's information requirements.

3.1.2. *Principle behind TARGETBUILDER system*

TARGETBUILDER enables users to compile a hierarchized list of actors (A) and of topics (T) to scan, build the target matrix itself and identify the A×T cells which represent "priority scanning areas" for the organization, for each A×T cell evaluate the organization's ability to "be informed early enough to make a decision", and for each specify the time scale relevance of the scan – i.e. whether it relates to the short-, medium- or long-term.

Figure 3.2 illustrates the position of TARGETBUILDER within the generic model of the process of anticipative strategic scanning.

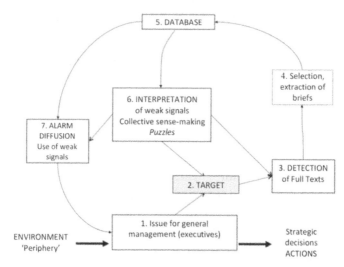

Figure 3.2. *Position of TARGETBUILDER in the process*

3.1.2.1. *Steps of use of TARGETBUILDER*

The steps involved in the process of targeting using TARGETBUILDER are modeled in Figure 3.3:

– delimiting the *domain of activity* of the organization that needs to be the focus of the anticipative strategic scanning (1). For example, in Figures 3.4–3.6, the domain of activity to scan was "sustainable logistics";

– identifying the *topics* (2) and *actors* (4) in the environment that are *relevant* to the domain of activity to scan;

– with regard to each topic (3) and each actor (5) identified above qualifying its level of *perceived importance*, on a scale of 1–4.

When they exist or can be established by the animator beforehand, *suggestive lists* of actors and topics can also be used as *input* to trigger collective thinking (see section 3.1.2.1):

– *filtering the lists* of actors (A) and topics (T) on the basis of the level of *perceived importance* and *cross-referencing* the filtered actors and topics to create an A×T matrix (6) for the complete target matrix (see Figure 3.5):

– identifying and selecting the *relevant A×T pairs* in that matrix (7);

– for each A×T pair selected, evaluating the organization's *anticipatory capacity*, i.e. its capacity to be informed early enough about that pair (green = satisfactory capacity, orange = room for improvement, red = unsatisfactory capacity (for a color version of the figure, see www.iste.co.uk/lesca/strategicdecisions.zip)) (8) and the *time scale relevance* of the scan for that pair, depending on whether it relates to changes or decisions to come in the short-, medium- or long-term (9);

– filtering the A×T pairs on the basis of the desired level of priority (importance of the actors/topics × anticipatory capacity × time scale relevance) in order to *zoom in* on the *priority target matrix* (see Figure 3.6).

At any moment, it is possible to *zoom out* to get back to:

– a broader list of actors and topics and adjust those lists or modify the level of perceived importance of an actor or topic;

– a broader target and adjust the priority target matrix.

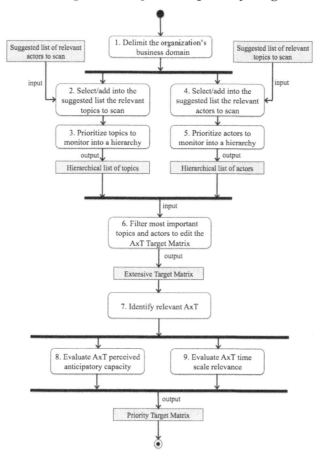

Figure 3.3. *Model of the method of targeting using TARGETBUILDER*

3.1.2.2. *Use of suggestive lists of actors and topics as the input for the targeting step*

TARGETBUILDER also enables us to use *suggestive lists* of actors and topics as the *input* to initiate and stimulate collective targeting. Notably, these lists can be built, before the targeting activity, on the basis of three aspects:

– *referential frames* of actors or stakeholders and topics, which cover part of the field of the overall issue on which the organization wishes to focus its effort in anticipative strategic scanning;

– lists of actors and topics related to the organization's strategic objectives and the managers' fields. Such lists are often fragmented, specialized in terms of fields, disseminated through the departments and not greatly formalized;

– APROXIMA (section 3.2) and ALHENA (section 3.3) can both help to supplement and adjust these suggestive lists with new actors and topics, which are within the organization's peripheral vision but which were not yet known to or clearly identified by the managers.

Together, these systems help in the gradual building of suggestive lists of actors and topics which, if they exist, could be used as *input* to:

– help *trigger* reflection about the information requirements of the anticipative strategic scanning;

– draw the managers' *attention* to actors and topics from the suggestive lists that they might not have thought of, had they not been suggested to them;

– trigger *surprises* and *discussions* between the participants about the relevance of certain actors and topics for the anticipative strategic scanning;

– bring new actors and/or topics to light in the discussion, which are not suggested by the lists and which have hitherto been hidden in the managers' *peripheral vision*.

This requires the *animator* of the scanning to make an effort in terms of preparation before the targeting session, drawing together these lists if they exist, supplementing them, structuring them and importing them into the system.

3.1.2.3. *Output produced with TARGETBUILDER*

Suggestive lists of actors and topics related to the organization's domain of activity, its environment and its strategy, which can be (re)used to trigger reflection about the target for the next round of anticipative strategic scanning. Figure 3.4 shows extracts from two examples of suggestive lists of actors and topics on the subject of sustainable logistics.

Figure 3.4. *Examples of lists of actors and topics obtained with TARGETBUILDER. For a color version of the figure, see www.iste.co.uk / lesca / strategicdecisions.zip*

The *hierarchized lists* of relevant and important actors (A) and topics (T) enable us to (temporarily) focus the effort of anticipative strategic scanning on certain parts of the environment, in accordance with the organization's objectives and strategic priorities. In Figure 3.4, the hierarchized lists are obtained by using a filter to *zoom in* on the actors and topics deemed to be most important on a scale of 1–4, represented by a green histogram.

The *target* itself is in the form of an *A×T matrix* where, for each A×T pair, the following aspects are specified:

– the *relevance of the A×T pair* for the organization, and therefore the importance of targeting the scan at that pair (this corresponds to "selection of A×T" in Figure 3.5);

– the *time scale relevance* of the A×T pair for the scan, depending on whether it relates to potential changes or decisions in the short-, medium- or long-term (this corresponds to "time scale relevance for A×T" in Figure 3.5);

– the *perceived anticipatory capacity*, i.e. the perceived capacity of the managers to be informed sufficiently early to "see changes coming" and anticipate the changes and decisions relating to that A×T pair (this corresponds to a color code in the cells in Figure 3.5: green indicates a satisfactory anticipatory capacity, orange indicates a capacity that needs improvement and red indicates a so-called "blindspot").

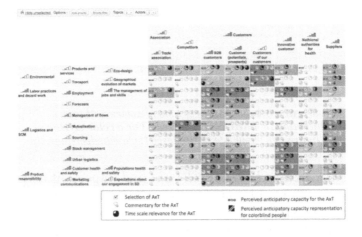

Figure 3.5. *Example of A×T target matrix obtained using TARGETBUILDER. For a color version of the figure, see www.iste.co.uk / lesca / strategicdecisions.zip*

The *priority target* (see Figure 3.6) is obtained by using filters to *zoom in* on:

– the most *important* actors and topics from the respective lists. Thus, users are able to focus their attention on those actors and topics to build the A×T target;

– the A×T pairs of *highest priority* in terms of their time scale relevance (short-, medium- or long-term) and perceived anticipatory capacity for the organization. This enables us to adjust the scope of the target, so it is "neither too broad nor too narrow" to prevent information overload and "blindness" of the anticipative strategic scanning.

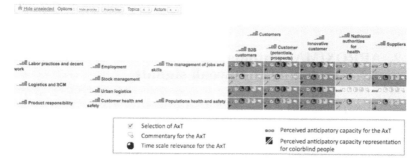

Figure 3.6. *Example of a priority matrix obtained with TARGETBUILDER. For a color version of the figure, see www.iste.co.uk / lesca / strategicdecisions.zip*

Step -by -step, the *traces* of the deliberations during the working session can be recorded in the form of *comments* associated with each actor, topic or A×T cell.

3.1.3. *Recap on TARGETBUILDER*

TARGETBUILDER is a system that aids in the collective building of a target for anticipative strategic scanning, comprising a list of actors (A), a list of topics (T) and the A×T matrix.

The matrix can be used to draw up an overall image of the information requirements held by the participants in the collective building session.

With TARGETBUILDER, it is also possible to prioritize the actors and topics. This function enables us to *zoom in* and adjust the scope of the target so it is "neither too broad nor too narrow" to prevent information overload and "blindness" of the anticipative strategic scanning.

By identifying the A×T pairs for which the organization's anticipatory capacity is insufficient, we have a relevant and useful starting point from which to *initiate* anticipative strategic scanning.

3.2. APROXIMA, automated extraction of fragments (briefs), which may hold weak signals

3.2.1. *Usefulness*

APROXIMA is the system to directly extract the anticipative briefs, which can be used by the hierarchy to make decisions quickly. In the process of anticipative strategic scanning, the use of APROXIMA requires the scanning target to have already been built. Its use is oriented toward the search for and exploitation of digital data obtained through the Internet. The volume of such data collections is increasing (referred to as "big data"), meaning that a system such as this has become absolutely crucial.

3.2.2. *Principle behind APROXIMA system*

APROXIMA detects full texts, extracts briefs and distributes those briefs in real time to the appropriate people. Figure 3.7 illustrates where APROXIMA fits into the generic model of the process of anticipative strategic scanning.

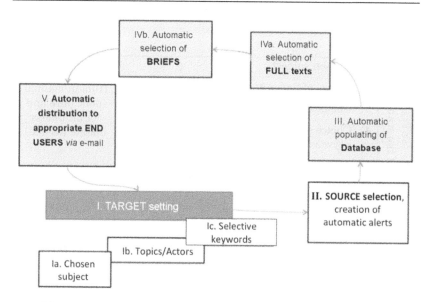

Figure 3.7. *Generic model of scanning process with APROXIMA*

3.2.2.1. *Steps of use of APROXIMA*

The setting up of the system requires human/manual intervention, which is easy to perform:

Ia) build the embryo of a scanning target (this will evolve later on);

Ib) name a few actors and topics already known to you, which relate to the target domain (e.g. solar/PV power).

Optional: draw up the list of authorized end users, and the list of actors and topics that are relevant to each of those users;

Ic) define and load the provisional pre-known *selective* words (the list will evolve later on, on the basis of feedback and experience), to detect the target texts;

Id) define and load the *anticipative* words and *verbs*. The list evolves on the basis of feedback.

List of steps during use of APROXIMA		Nature of the steps
SETTING of the scan target	1) Chosen subject 2) Choice of topics and actors to target 3) Choice of *language* 4) Choice of *selective* and *anticipative* keywords 5) Selection of information sources (Internet)	Human/manual (done once and for all unless update needed)
EXPLOITATION (automated)	6) *Collection of full texts* and storage in the database 7) Automatic selection of FULL texts 8) Automatic selection of BRIEFS 9) V. Automatic *distribution* to the relevant END USERS in view of their focus of interest, by e-mail	*Automated*

Table 3.1. *Steps in the use of APROXIMA*

Anticipative words (examples)	Anticipative verbs (examples)
Alliance, hiring, laboratory, nomination, partnership, possible, potential, project, prototype, replacement, researcher, resignation, start-up, sudden departure, university, etc.	Beginning, constructing, creating, developing, envisaging, harnessing, hiring, integrating, launching, naming, putting in place, removing, replacing, resigning, updating, etc.

Table 3.2. *Examples of "anticipative" words and verbs*

II) choose the digital information sources. Two types of sources are used in the present case: those that can be accessed automatically by FACTIVA and newspapers' websites that are relevant but inaccessible to FACTIVA, such as the newspaper *Le Monde*.

Thereafter, the operations take place automatically:

III) APROXIMA *automatically* collects *full texts*. It stores them in its database;

IVa) APROXIMA *automatically* extracts and "cleans up" the full texts as such (it removes purely technical traces). It stores them in its database;

IVb) APROXIMA *automatically* filters and stores the relevant *briefs*. There is a reference from each brief to the full text from which it came;

V) APROXIMA *automatically sends an alert* in real time to any and all people authorized, about the new *briefs* produced corresponding to each person's profile.

3.2.2.2. *Output produced by APROXIMA*

The output automatically generated by APROXIMA is as follows:

– the *metrics* of the scanning result: number of full texts detected, number of briefs selected and number of full texts that contained one or more briefs;

– the full texts detected;

– the automatically selected *briefs*;

[31]. The ***photo*voltaic industry will represent 15% of European electrical production by 2030, or 25% "if there is a paradigm shift"**, according to a report from EPIA[http://www.connectingthesun.eu/report/reports/], published Wednesday 17 October

Figure 3.8. *Example of a brief obtained using APROXIMA*

– the *alert messages* automatically sent by APROXIMA to the mobile phones of the authorized end users.

Figure 3.9. *Example of an alert message sent by APROXIMA to a mobile phone (search performed in Spanish by a Colombian ministry). For a color version of the figure, see www.iste.co.uk / lesca / strategicdecisions.zip*

– the *summary of briefs* sent automatically to subscribers. The summary is the collection and presentation of briefs on a given topic over a predefined period of time. The summary is formatted and then automatically e-mailed to the authorized subscribers.

Figure 3.10. *Example of summary of three briefs (search performed in Spanish by a Colombian ministry). For a color version of the figure, see www.iste.co.uk / lesca / strategicdecisions.zip*

3.2.3. Case study: application to the topic of "solar/photovoltaic" power

3.2.3.1. *Organization's issue*

The CEO is wondering about the possibility, for his organization, of involving itself in the sector of solar energy. He is aware that there are major difficulties in this sector on an international scale, and that its medium- and long-term future does not look promising at the moment. However, he thinks the future could, in fact, be different. Therefore, he wishes to gather elements of ideas and put them to the board of directors.

With this goal in mind, he asks the animator of the anticipative strategic scanning to look for information useful in guiding the thought process. To begin with, he specifies that the initial search will be limited to digital sources, written in French. It will be limited to a recent and short period of time, merely for exploratory purposes.

3.2.3.2. *Use of APROXIMA*

The animator thus makes use of APROXIMA in the following way:

– timespan: 18 February–18 June 2013;

– selective words: *photovoltaïque* (photovoltaic) and *solaire* (solar). These are the generic topics of the scan target;

– sources consulted: FACTIVA and the newspapers *Le Monde*, *Libération* and *Le Figaro*.

3.2.3.3. *Output automatically generated by APROXIMA*

The results comprise the following elements:

– metrics;

Metrics	Results
Number of *full texts* detected	651
Number of briefs extracted (see example below)	567 (~1–4 lines in length)
Number of *full texts* from which one or more briefs have been extracted	322
Number of *full texts* that produced no briefs	329

Table 3.3. *Examples of metrics*

– the briefs themselves;

Results for topic 'Solaire'. Date: 29/11/2011 09:56:40 am	
Selective words: energ, photovolt, solaire	
Sources	Briefs
......	......
UE/ÉNERGIE: plan solaire méditerranéen, un cap est franchi (25/11/2011) *Source: AEFR*	Siemens, ABB et Deutsche Bank, rejoints en 2010 par l'italien Enel Green Power, le français Saint-Gobain Solar, l'espagnol Red Electrica et le marocain Nareva Holding, Desertec est un projet de réseau de centrales <u>solaires et fermes éoliennes dans le nord de l'Afrique et au Moyen-Orient, qui veut couvrir jusqu'à 15% des besoins de l'UE en électricité d'ici 2025.</u> View Content <u>ENVJOB [ENVJOB] - Nouvelle ENR : " Le tiers financement est l'avenir du photovoltaïque"</u>
Le projet solaire géant Desertec a trouvé son réseau (24/11/2011) *Source: FIGARO*	Pourquoi les pays d'Afrique du Nord devraient-ils exporter de l'électricité alors que leurs besoins énergétiques progressent plus vite encore que leur <u>croissance économique ? "Vendre leurs kilowattheures à un bon prix aux Européens permet par la suite de faire baisser le prix du courant sur le marché intérieur" , explique Cédric Philibert, chargé de l'énergie solaire</u> à l'Agence internationale de l'énergie (AIE). <u>View Content</u>
OFFRES DES PAYS DE LA RIVE SUD DE LA MÉDITERRANÉE (24/11/2011) *Source: EURPTQ*	L'ambition du Maroc est de produire d'ici 2020 des fermes solaires d'une capacité totale de 2 GW. <u>View Content</u>

Table 3.4. *Examples of briefs*

– the full texts from which the briefs were extracted. To obtain the full text, users need only click on the underlined hyperlink ("View Content") following the brief.

The animator gives the list of briefs to the CEO. What happens next? Here is the most usual scenario.

3.2.3.4. *Examples of reactions from managers*

The CEO reads through the list of briefs. His attention is drawn to some of them in particular, possibly because a contradiction is immediately apparent, or because one of them triggers an idea, etc.

EXAMPLE 3.1.–

"A *contradiction* which draws the attention: the Swiss competitor ABB is acting in an unexpected manner":

– on the one hand, there are numerous records of bankruptcy and abandoned projects by organizations in the PV sector;

– on the other hand, the Swiss group ABB is buying up competitors who are on the verge of bankruptcy.

> *ABB 7 briefs* express the strategy of the ABB Group in the PV sector and for the future, in spite of the "volatility" of that sector – for instance:

> [261]. "ABB has bought out Power-One for 1 billion USD. The company admitted that the photovoltaic market was likely to remain volatile in the short term: 2013 will be a difficult year."

> [266]. "...the directors of *ABB* remain confident in the future of photovoltaic... confirming the group's intention to place renewable energy at the very heart of its strategy."

> [454]. "Photovoltaic energy; *ABB anticipates a revival...*"

This apparent contradiction causes questions to begin being asked: what is the strategy being exercised by our competitor, ABB? Should we draw inspiration from them, or should we, in fact, stay on our guard? What will the International Energy Agency (IEA)'s forthcoming report (26/06/2013) say? etc.

In mid-June 2013, the animator of the anticipative strategic scanning brought the following brief to the attention of the hierarchy: *"ABB Surprise resignation* of the CEO (Joe Hogan) of the Swiss giant ABB Group [...] The news has taken all analysts entirely by surprise [...] During his 'reign', Joe Hogan increased the corporation's turnover from 35 billion to 39.3 billion dollars" [BER 13].

EXAMPLE 3.2.–Energy management of buildings: would this be a promising area for us?

> [157]. *"... Saint-Gobain Solar*: 'We need to bring photovoltaic energy into the mains grid of the *building*', confides one of the organization's managers."

> [275]. "The inverter is only one part of what they are offering, alongside communication, monitoring and supervision systems, connecting boxes, electrical devices, electrical security and surveillance systems, transformers and delivery stations, etc. 'Our position on the photovoltaic market relates to all of electrical conversion', points out Ignace de Prest, from *Schneider Electric*."

The construction of all sorts of buildings has a very bright future in many countries: China, Indonesia, the Middle East, etc. The potential markets are enormous. Should we take an interest in this area? Schneider Electric is already capitalizing, but there should be room for us as well: almost everything still remains to be done in this domain. Could Schneider be a potential partner for us?

EXAMPLE 3.3.–"Innovating to find an answer to a crucial question: how can we store electricity? Electricity storage is a dream in most countries, but it is one we are not able to deliver at present. Anyone who finds an acceptable economic solution will have many excellent business opportunities."

Should we orientate our "RADAR" toward laboratories and start-ups working in this field?

3.2.4. *Recap on APROXIMA*

APROXIMA enables users to quickly circumvent the problem of information overload with textual data obtained from the Internet:

– it directly provides briefs a few lines long selected on the basis of the selective words input at the beginning. These briefs can be used directly for collective creation of meaning sessions (e.g. using the Puzzle method);

– it only gives anticipative briefs, if we want it to.

In addition, with APROXIMA, it is possible to tweak the anticipative strategic scanning target: on reading the briefs obtained after an extraction, users will realize that certain full texts selected in fact hold no interest. In discovering why they hold no interest, we can pick "selective" words to filter out, so the program will no longer select a full text containing one of those words. This feedback operation is highly useful in dealing with information overload. Figure 3.11 illustrates the process.

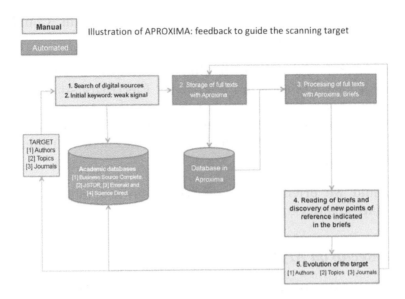

Figure 3.11. *Feedback into targeting process*

3.3. ALHENA, an aid to finding connections between weak signals

3.3.1. *Usefulness*

ALHENA is able to detect full texts that have elements in common. Those elements could be identical words, but also synonyms. The full texts sharing elements are referred to as "adjacent information". Adjacent information fragments are grouped together and presented in the form of a graph, appropriately known as a "constellation". Automated adjacency detection applied to raw data helps identify any possible connections between the information fragments.

The concept of "adjacent information" is useful when comparing two (or more) pieces of information not necessarily written in identical words. The aim of the comparison is to:

– lend credibility to one (or several) of the texts;

– supplement information lacking from one (or several) of them with information from the other(s);

– demonstrate an inconsistency or contradiction between two pieces of information;

– facilitate the interpretation of that information set;

– reveal a new extension of the initial issue;

– envisage links between pieces of information (complementarity, inconsistency, contradiction, etc.). Examples are given in the case study.

Figure 3.12 shows the position of ALHENA in the generic model of the process of anticipative strategic scanning.

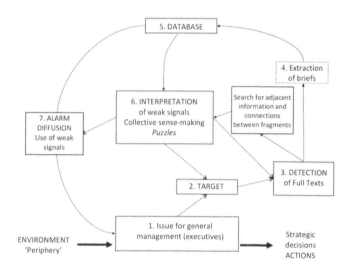

Figure 3.12. *Position of ALHENA*

3.3.2. *Principle behind ALHENA system*

3.3.2.1. *Steps of use of ALHENA*

Full texts that are relevant to the organization's issue are fed into ALHENA. These texts will have been selected beforehand (possibly by APROXIMA, for example). They are provided in an unordered form. There may be several hundred of them at a time.

The full texts are automatically processed by ALHENA. The duration of the processing step may be between one and several hours, without human intervention, depending on the number of *full texts*. All the full texts will be written in the same language.

3.3.2.2. *Output generated by ALHENA*

The output is given in visual form of drawings; an example is given in Table 3.5. The adjacent information fragments are grouped together on the computer screen. Each of them is represented by a number, assigned by ALHENA. There will be as many groups as there are "clusters" of adjacent information fragments. In view of its appearance, a group is known as a "constellation".

Generally, the processing step yields more than one group (or constellation). The whole of the graphic result is called a "galaxy" because of its similarity in appearance to a starry night sky. Each full text belongs to one, and only one, constellation.

If we click on its number, the full text is displayed on the screen, along with information helpful to the user (an example is shown in Figure 3.12).

3.3.3. *Case study: application to the topic of "CO_2 valorization"*

3.3.3.1. *Organization's issue*

The directors of the organization "Durability" (chemical sector) decided to explore the possibility of exploiting CO_2 as a primary material with the aim of diversifying the organization's activities in a strategic orientation for the future. A think-tank session of the board of directors was convened. The subject on the day's agenda was: "to explore the possibility and financial relevance of valorizing CO_2 as a potential primary material".

The person (called the animator) in charge of preparing the full texts likely to be used for the next board meeting gathered 299 full texts that might be applicable to the issue at hand, but it is impossible for that person to read all of the texts in the short time available (raw data overload).

In order to prepare for the meeting, the animator must perform the following tasks:

– search for and extract the full texts potentially applicable to the topic at hand, and likely to contain possible anticipative information signaling changes in the organization's relevant environment. By scanning a number of sources (using APROXIMA), the animator was, in this case, able to gather 299 full texts;

– evaluate the degree of *reliability* of each text;

– refer backward and forward numerous times from one full text to another to guide the participants in their reflections and interactions during the meeting.

Here are some examples of interactions, recorded during previous sessions attended by the animator:

VERBATIM 3.1.– (interactions between participants in a collective creation of meaning session)

"*Comparing* this piece of information with that one makes me think that…"

"Those two pieces of adjacent information seem to be *inconsistent*, unless…"

"What you're saying certainly *fits in* well with what's on the screen... it's the missing link between the two pieces of information..."

"There is, however, something, which should suggest that..."

"Looking at what we've written on the screen, I remember that last week, someone told me that..."

"We need to look for ... to supplement the information..."

"Are we certain that the information we're discussing here is *reliable?*"

"Do we already have any "adjacent" information for this – anything which could *back it up?*"

Constraints/time pressure.– The CEO insisted that the full texts be prepared in as short a time as possible in order to reduce administration costs and increase the organization's reactivity. He had already declared: "Unless a significant time gain is made, the strategic scanning will be abandoned!"

Hope/hypothesis.– It would be very helpful to divide the 299 full texts into small groups of "adjacent" information (these groups are called "local constellations") demonstrating the cases above.

This is precisely what the ALHENA system allows us to do.

3.3.3.2. *Preparation for board of directors session*

A collective reflection session, bringing together many members of the board of directors, was convened. The agenda was framed as: "To explore the possibility and financial relevance of valorizing CO_2 as a potential primary material". For the meeting, therefore, the animator needs to be able to:

– present the full texts selected, if necessary, in as visual a manner as possible;

– respond very quickly to any requests the participants may make as the meeting proceeds;

– without interfering with the rhythm of the participants' interactions, accompany the discussion with a projection of the full texts which may aid in the collective reflection;

– respond, quickly and as and when required, to any questions such as: "Is this information reliable? Do we have any other information that could supplement it? Does any of our other information contradict or undermine it? etc."

The ALHENA system was designed and built with a view to providing an efficient aid to fulfilling such conditions.

3.3.3.3. *Visual output generated by ALHENA*

ALHENA displays the visual representation shown in Figure 3.13. The diagram shown here is reminiscent of a "global galaxy", in which the 299 full texts are identifiable by their number. The animator sees three types of graphical shapes:

– double-ended arrows indicating the position of the "nuclei";

– small *local constellations* centered at their nucleus (a set of double-ended arrows);

– *local constellation arms* – arms made up of series of *full texts* connected by single arrows.

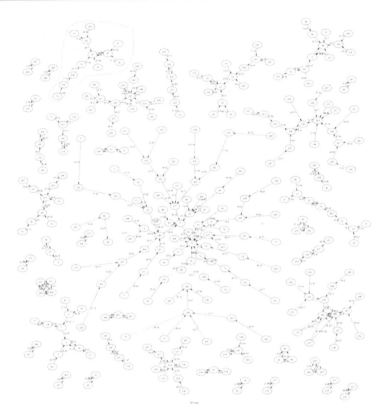

Figure 3.13. *Output from ALHENA: global galaxy made up of various local constellations, one of which is circled here (top left, in red in the color version). For a color version of the figure, see www.iste.co.uk / lesca / strategicdecisions.zip*

3.3.3.4. *Use of output by the animator*

The steps taken by the animator are as follows. First, the animator clicks on a local constellation, which we will denote as LC (for example, the LC circled and centered at the nucleus 45–47 in Figure 3.13). He obtains:

– a page with the graphic representation of the local constellation;

– the table showing the word cloud for the local constellation.

The word cloud for the local constellation gives the animator a general idea about its subject. The word clouds on the branches give the animator an indication of the way in which the subject is dealt with in each of them.

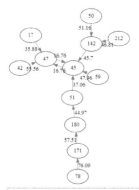

biocarburants *bactérique* biodiésel *budget captage carbonne* cecr cellulosique *charbon chauge chef créée* devoir dollar *déchet* enerkem *estrie état europe européen financement* gaz *greencentre* greenfield greenline *génération inc. industries* innovation *kingston* leaf *maroc norme* papetier *pays* production produire produit recherche science *stockage* synthèse *tournes* tunis tunisie tunisien *université* usine *étape éthanol*	

47,142,212,45,	*action agnin munnu ni nowe bua biocarburants reach* captage carburant cellulosique *charbon chef oil innovati concemer voir* devoir *donnur évpertum dépendures ampre* enerkem *exprimes plus pi provunation* greenfield *groupe aiome immunisant les savoni* norme *obama ontario* production *produue* propre *apper* renouvelable *réduire secure* stockage stratégie *tachnologia* usine énergie éthanol
47,51,180,78,171,45,	*anne avenu barnburan budget mois* cecr cellulosique *chage def* chimique *éhuage* créer devoir dollar enerkem entreprise estrie état europe européen *exuple* *expertise exportation* financements greencentre greenfield *innovatun* innovation *jeune* kingston maroc *mondial pays politique* production *public plus* recherche *relance* science technologique *tourner* tunis tunisie tunisien *unirsita uine* éthanol *étranger*
47,45,17,	*un anne un* biocarburants *biodimique un caubols un un* carburant cellulosique *um* chef chimique *un* conditionné *un deux* déchet *économi* enerkem *exploiter la* gaz *pi* greenfield *génération matière mondial ontario* production produire produit *pollet renovuble reduce obe* société synthèse *technoloque* usine *vri venaux vecoburg* étape éthanol *émine ilot*
47,50,142,45,	*un marime an es opnen sum* biocarburants *budget* bret *une* mali *order un sum* cellulosique *une def un un immunal* concerner *auome avenus* dollar *déja éspratune* enerkem *une limique pi gant* greenfield *amont* *ontario* papetier *papu pouroi* production *propu sepui* recherche *sature sonte souite soin soula technique* usine *uage* éthanol
47,59,45,	*um uun un us s univum eno a suu* biocarburants *sumul leulo sunite* space *unun uum* cellulosique *un chef un sum immunal sungue sanpu sungem um us* enerkem *amropia bolilia pi* greenfield *prodnum souvu retaru* organique *parte proms* production *paps monte* shetberobe *uuns wchuonga technlogu wlphau* usine *aquepuct* éthanol
47,42,45,	*un un un sum un uum sum* biodiésel *un un uum un un pi* cellulosique *un un du som omnunol augas um un* energy enerkem *somemus pi* greenfield greenline *inc.* industries *ummum um* leaf *un mnovil* *omum pm pm* production *papu chum unun uuaungn* usine énergie éthanol

Table 3.5. *Information in local constellation centered at 45-47. For a color version of the figure, see www.iste.co.uk / lesca / strategicdecisions.zip*

The animator need only read the text of the nucleus:

– either to decide to give-up on reading all the full texts in the constellation: this represents a time gain, and a reduction in overload;

– or to be alerted to the usefulness of reading at least the full texts in the initial corona around the nucleus: this increases the attention paid to these texts.

3.3.3.4.1. Nucleus

The animator first points to one of the nuclei.

Let us take the example of the double-ended arrow connecting the full texts 45–47, at the center of the constellation ringed in Figure 3.13.

He sees that each of the arrows has a number. This number is the same – in this case, "16.76", for both arrows. It is the smallest number in the local constellation, so 45 and 47 are the most closely adjacent as defined above. Indeed, this is a general property: the nucleus always gives us the smallest measurement in each local constellation.

The animator clicks on 45:

– instantly, the main keywords in full text 45 are displayed in the top left-hand box, while the full text is displayed in the bottom left-hand box;

– full text 47 is displayed on the right, with the main keywords in the top box and the full text in the bottom one.

Thus, the animator is able to compare texts 45 and 47 if he needs to (see Figure 3.14). The comparison is facilitated by the fact that the words common to texts 45 and 47 are highlighted in salmon pink by ALHENA. If there are synonyms, these are shown in blue (for a color version of the figure, see www.iste.co.uk/lesca/strategicdecisions.zip), while any co-occurrences of words are underlined.

Surprise.– In the second row, the software displays the words most commonly occurring in the two texts. In this case, these words are: "Enerkem", "GreenField" (both actors in the chemical industry), "éthanol" and "cellulosique" (cellulosic [relating to or derived from cellulose]). The participants, the members of the board of directors, ask themselves: might Enerkem and GreenField, whom no one has so far mentioned at Durability, be potential competitors for us, of whom we were not aware, with regard to the strategic path of "CO$_2$ valorization" being explored here?

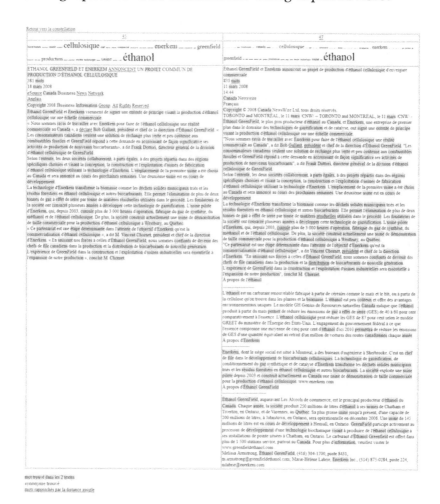

Figure 3.14. *Visualization and comparison between texts 45 and 47 in the nucleus. For a color version of the figure, see www.iste.co.uk / lesca / strategicdecisions.zip*

Other observations:

– 45 and 47 have many words in common, but they are not duplicates, as they do not have the same *number of words* (381 for text 45 and 835 for text 47); their *original sources* are not the same, and neither are their *dates of publication* (11 March 2008 for 47 and 18 March for 45). The animator may suggest that 45 and 47 give one another credibility, or at least that they significantly *confirm* one another.

– Durability is exploring the possibility of valorizing CO_2 by producing ethanol using algae. However, in these texts, cellulosic ethanol is mentioned: could this be a competitive avenue... using a *competitive technology*? Does Durability need to worry about this? The Attention is *alerted* to issues that the managers might not yet have considered.

In summary:

– the system draws attention to the entry points in the 299 full texts: the nuclei of the local constellations;

– if we point to a nucleus, the system suggests numerous elements to feed into the strategic thinking of Durability's board of directors;

– the time needed is very short in comparison to what it would have been if the animator had had to do everything manually. The time gain is a convincing argument in the eyes of the hierarchy (because of the cost reduction). Yet this is by no means the only contribution made by the ALHENA system.

3.3.3.4.2. Small corona around the nucleus

The animator wonders whether the information fragments 45/47 could be supplemented or rendered more reliable. Therefore, he examines the full texts making up the near corona around 45/47 in the constellation displayed on the screen: 51, 142, 17, 42 and 59. By clicking, one-by-one, on each of these numbers, the full texts appear, as do the most frequently occurring words, shown in the second row (see Figure 3.14).

The animator can very quickly see that all the texts in the corona of the 45/47 nucleus (except for 42) provide elements of additional information about the actors "Enerkem" and "GreenField", on the one hand, and the topic "cellulosic ethanol", on the other. These additional elements can therefore help to reassure the board members about the reliability of texts 45/47. They may also draw their vigilance to the potential competitors Enerkem and Greenfield because neither these actors nor the topic of "cellulosic ethanol" was included in the initial anticipative strategic scanning target.

3.3.3.4.3. Constellation arm

The participants may ask the animator why full texts are connected to one another to form a local constellation arm. For example, 78, 171, 180 and 51 constitute the longest arm of the local constellation 45/47. If the animator clicks on 78, ALHENA displays the full texts 78 and 171. It also indicates: the words common to the two texts (highlighted in salmon pink); synonyms and any co-occurrences (as mentioned previously). Then, the animator can click on 171, for example, this displays texts 171 and 180, and so on until the nucleus is reached.

The texts we pass through on the journey from the outer end of a local constellation arm toward its nucleus will be increasingly short, and the main keywords will play an increasingly important relative role: in this particular case, those words are "Enerkem" and "cellulosic ethanol".

3.3.3.4.4. Summary

For the above explanations, we chose to use information fragments 45/47, connected by a double-ended arrow and situated at the center of a local constellation (see Table 3.5). Thus, we have been able to demonstrate that the existence of a local constellation such as this is capable of drawing attention to a sub-issue which might not have been mentioned previously by Durability's directors, but which may cause a reaction when discovered. The hierarchy's "field of vision" is increased, where previously there was a blindspot. Yet the global galaxy contains other local constellations which need to be examined in the same way.

An examination of all the nuclei in the global galaxy (see Figure 3.13) was made by the animator during his preparation. The time required was approximately 2 h: 1 h of the program running (without human intervention) followed by 1 h of "human work" for the animator to analyze the galaxy. The result was that only one other nucleus also appeared to be possibly interest-worthy: the nucleus 70/73, which draws the attention to the "food industry" avenue for CO_2 valorization. When pursued, this avenue caused surprise amongst the board of directors: it had never previously been mentioned. The following strategic questions were raised: "Should we take an interest in this area? Are there already serious competitors at work in this field? Should we consider going into partnerships? What results could this produce over the course of the next decade? etc."

3.3.3.5. *Recap on the ALHENA system*

The hypothesis about the usefulness of a system such as ALHENA has gone a long way toward validation by replication of the approach used in this experiment in new fields of application.

The application made of ALHENA shows us that the animator need only read the text of the nucleus:

– either to decide to give-up on reading all the full texts in the constellation: this represents a time gain, and a *reduction in overload*;

– or to be alerted to the usefulness of reading at least the full texts in the initial corona around the nucleus: this *increases the attention* paid to these texts.

In addition, ALHENA provides an answer to the question "How can we *Zoom in*" suggested by Moss Kanter (see Chapter 2) and how to expand the field of peripheral vision and thus discover any existing blindspots.

VERBATIM 3.2.– (examples of reactions from the board of directors)

"A huge body of full texts is replaced by a figure which fits on one page or on the projector screen. This changes everything – it's much easier to use!"

"The simple fact that we immediately know which full texts have elements in common with which other full texts already helps to make sense of what was, previously, just a mountain of raw data."

"Visualization immediately triggers reflection."

"I have the feeling of navigating at a variety of altitudes with this possibility of zooming in and out."

3.4. Conclusion

This chapter has introduced three systems designed to resolve a hitherto-unresolved question about the process of anticipative strategic scanning: how can we provide an aid to the detection of weak signals, which could help managers to formulate anticipation useful for strategic decision-making?

The system, TARGETBUILDER helps target information in anticipative strategic scanning in accordance with the strategic objectives set by the hierarchy. It is used in meeting rooms during collective work bringing together the organization's managers. The aim of the meeting is to specify which elements of the organization's environment (i.e. which actors and/or topics), whose decisions and/or evolutions it would be helpful to anticipate, are relevant. The program helps to build an evolving target that is neither too restrictive nor too vast.

APROXIMA enables us to directly obtain briefs, i.e. information fragments likely to be interpreted as possible weak signals. APROXIMA performs four tasks:

– consultation of the digital information sources indicated to it;

– selection of the articles (in full text form) corresponding to the selective words input by the user;

– storage of the articles in its database;

– extraction of briefs (text fragments) in view of the selective words and anticipative words input by the user.

ALHENA processes a big volume of (say, a thousand) full texts that are fed into it to reveal groups of "adjacent" information fragments. The output is groups of information fragments presented in graphical form, called "local constellations". A local constellation contains all the full texts that deal with the same subject. The program helps to find links between full texts previously stored in an unordered form in the database (links such as confirmation and contradiction).

Conclusion

Chapter 1 demonstrated the importance of weak signals in the process of strategic decision-making in organizations. A particular characteristic of strategic decision-making is that it is orientated toward the future: it requires us to be able to anticipate. Weak signals, if they are detected and interpreted appropriately, are a way of anticipating. Anticipative strategic scanning is the process whereby weak signals are obtained. This process comprises detection, selection and interpretation of the weak signals. Yet each of these operations raises numerous operational difficulties, which are capable of dissuading the managers from making use of weak signals. These difficulties are compounded by the situation of *information overload* or *raw data overload*, which affect all organizations. The intense use of the Internet merely exacerbates the problem. The need for appropriate systems is apparent at every step in the process of anticipative strategic scanning.

Chapter 2 seeks to answer the question: have appropriate systems been proposed by authors writing in academic journals? The answer is only partially positive. The systems that have been proposed cover only one part of the anticipative strategic scanning process: particularly, the final part of the process regarding the interpretation of weak signals, as shown throughout the course of the chapter.

However, the most serious lacuna is this: *how are weak signals detected and extracted* in the context of information overload, which most frequently occurs in organizations?

Chapter 3 aims to answer this question. Three systems are presented. They were developed by academic researchers conducting their work in university laboratories and at the CNRS. Those three systems are the following:

– TARGETBUILDER, an aid to the targeting of anticipative strategic scanning. The objective is to determine the part of the environment that needs to be scanned in order to detect the weak signals, for which we will then search: the part which is not only as complete as possible but also as clearly delimited as possible (neither overly extensive nor overly restrictive), which should serve the managers' prioritized requirements. According to all hypotheses, the target must be able to evolve. The work that eventually birthed TARGETBUILDER initially set out to serve the needs of an organization in the field of logistics and sustainable development.

– APROXIMA, for detection and extraction of possible weak signals in big volumes of "raw" textual data (full texts) obtained from digital information sources using the Internet. The possible weak signals are fragments of text that are relevant in regard to criteria specified in advance. In particular, they must be *anticipative* in nature. The work that gave rise to APROXIMA was initially intended to satisfy the request of a ministry. APROXIMA is now being used in that ministry.

– ALHENA, to group together so-called "adjacent" information fragments in a big volume of full texts obtained from digital information sources on the Internet. Two pieces of information are said to be adjacent when they have a word (or several) in common. The adjacency score for two words results from a distance calculation. The output produced by

ALHENA is presented in the form of word clusters (or clouds). These clusters are useful when we are looking for possible links between pieces of information that are swamped in a big volume of data – e.g. links of confirmation, contradiction, etc. The work that produced ALHENA was originally intended toward serving the needs of ministries and banks, when they envisaged using the Puzzle method presented in Chapter 2.

Glossary

Actionable knowledge: refers to knowledge that can be used to act. It can take on various forms, for example a procedure, a method and an algorithm.

Actor: refers to a natural or legal person, external (sometimes internal) to the organization; whose decisions and actions could have an influence on the future of the organization or on activities for which it is responsible. Thus, actors to scan are not limited to competitors. They are closer to the notion of stakeholders.

Adjacent information: refers to two information items that relate to the same topic, but have few or no words in common (despite being written in the same language).

Animator: refers to the person tasked with running the strategic scanning process, "bringing it to life" and making it endure. Animator inaptitude is a factor of abandonment of strategic scanning.

Anticipation: refers to the process of imagining the sequences of possible consequences of an event that has been announced or barely started, and taking action before those consequences are realized, in order to influence their progress, take advantage of them or, alternatively, guard against them.

Anticipative information: refers to an information item, the interpretation of which suggests that an event could occur within a time horizon that is relevant to the person doing the interpreting. An anticipative information item enables a possible danger, or a potentially good business opportunity, to be "foreseen in advance".

Anticipative strategic scanning: refers to the collective and proactive process by which members of the company (or institution) track, on a voluntary basis, and use the relevant information concerning their external environment and the changes that could occur in it. ASS aims to innovate, stand out, react more quickly and adapt to the changing environment, to avoid unpleasant strategic surprises, to reduce risks and uncertainty in general.

Attention: refers to the ability of a person to direct and focus their mind on an event, an object or another person likely to constitute an informational clue.

Brief: refers to an information item reduced to its essential words so as to be very short. This size constraint results from the fact that a news brief is intended to be projected onto a screen (using a video projector, for example) along with other news briefs. The news briefs, thus brought together, help elicit meaning during a session of collective creation of meaning, using the Puzzle method. A news brief results from the extraction of a few essential words from a data item, typically a document, which may number several pages (full text).

Collective creation of meaning: refers to the operation of collective and debated interpretation during which "added meaning" and knowledge are created from weak signals, among others. Creation of meaning is arrived at through interactions, exteriorization of tacit knowledge and deliberations among the participants in the work session. The examined weak signals act as inducing *stimuli*.

Complex/complexity: refers to an entity comprising rather numerous and sometimes diverse elements as well as (many) relationships among those elements. Interactions can also occur with the entity's environment. Consequently, the notion of complexity implies that of unpredictable possibility, of plausible emergence of new things and meaning within the phenomenon that is considered complex.

Discontinuity: refers to the outbreak of an unexpected event, totally at odds with the extrapolations that could be made from the previous situation. Usually, discontinuity simply denotes the opposite of continuity, which is associated with the notion of continuum, whose origin is geometrical. Its meaning is close to that of a disruption.

Disruption: refers to a break in an element or in the flow of a process. It is synonymous with discontinuity.

Early warning: refers to a formal information item (in text form, provided by an electronic sensor, or the like), or to a sensory information item (visual or auditory observation, etc.) felt by a human being and leading to the thinking that a possible, relevant and significant "event" might occur within such a time horizon that there is still time for action, either to take advantage of the event or to guard against it (when it constitutes a risk, for example):

– putting ourselves in a position to pick up signals that we will interpret as being possible harbingers of a danger (or of a good opportunity), in order to prepare to act quickly and at the right time;

– creating the conditions or circumstances that will make it possible to act quickly and at the right time.

Early warning signal: refers to a signal that announces changes in the enterprise's environment, which might significantly influence its prospects. This usually results from the interpretation of a weak signal.

Environment: refers to all the actors and events that are likely to interact with an enterprise, at present or in the reasonable future, in accordance with its activities and businesses. This explains occasional references to current or potential actors current or potential clients, current or potential competitors, etc.

Environmental scanning: refers to "the monitoring, evaluating and disseminating of information to key managers within the organization" [AGU 67, p. 1]. "It is an important aspect of strategic management" [KUM 01, p. 1] "because it serves as the first link in the chain of perceptions and actions that permit an organization to adapt to its environment" [HAM 81, p. 299].

Filtering: an ambiguous term that can have either a positive or a negative connotation. Negative connotation means getting rid of some information items, which one does not wish to make known; a meaning that borders on "censorship". In some cases, filtering explains why the hierarchy "did not foresee anything" despite strong signals being sent to it. Positive connotation: isolating a relevant information item drowned in irrelevant data. Accordingly, we avoid the word "filtering" in this book.

Focused search: refers to a method of information acquisition that takes place when managers are already involved in a decision-making process, and are looking for information to better understand the decision context, choices and implications. First, a situation that must be decided on is identified, questions are raised and asked, and then a focused search is engaged. The objective is to find and gather reliable and non-ambiguous information to give as precise and clear answers as possible to the manager's questions. Thus, information evaluation is both analytic and deductive.

Full text: designates a data item generally presented in the form of text, or a table, whose length may vary from a few lines to several full pages.

Information: refers to all or part of a raw data item, which, on examination, turns out to be of interest, Such interest can be justified by means of explicit criteria. Also denotes an observation conducted in the field.

Information overload: is a multidimensional construct, consisting of three components: (1) equivocality, (2) quantity and (3) variety. Equivocality refers to the existence of multiple valid interpretations of information; quantity measures the volume and availability of information, while variety measures the different sources of information. Equivocality refers to the existence of multiple valid interpretations of information.

Noise: refers to the fact that a relevant information item is drowned out inside a large volume of irrelevant data. The relevant information item may well go unnoticed; much like a voice can be inaudible in a very noisy setting.

Perception: refers to sensory information. One of our senses (or several at the same time) delivers an immediate information item to us. For example, during an important meeting, I perceive that the manager has a slight smirk when one of the collaborators says something. This visual sensory information could instantaneously "tell me a lot".

Peripheral vision: refers, in the context of this book, to the ability to see somewhat more than meets the eye. When one is presented with a written information item, being able to see only that item is evidence of very weak peripheral vision. Conversely, being able to also see other, related information items, either actual or retrieved from memory, is evidence of a certain degree of peripheral vision.

Puzzle: refers to a justified graphical construction, comprising a small number of information fragments pertaining to a common set of issues (agent and/or topic) and deemed able to enrich one another.

Puzzle method: refers to a method for exploiting weak-signal type information. A weak signal, considered in isolation, is rarely meaningful, exceptions aside. The Puzzle method helps bring several fragmentary information items together and interpret them to create meaning. The idea is to draw formal information items as well as tacit ones (the latter, however, being spontaneously expressed on the spot), along with formal and tacit knowledge, to derive conclusions that lead to action to be taken. Practicing this method gives rise to the construction of graphical representations, also called Puzzle (by analogy with the homonymous game). The Puzzle method is more fruitful when used within a group for collective creation of meaning.

Raw data: refers to a text or image (on paper, digital medium or electronic messaging), alternatively to a sound recording, which reaches us without us voluntarily seeking it. A raw data item can also result from a search performed with keywords (sometimes referred to as *Full text*). It may prove to be of no interest (*Raw data*). But it may also turn out to contain a weak signal lost in the volume like "a needle in a haystack".

Reactivity: refers to the ability to act either as a result of an event that has already happened or as a result of a sign that foretells an event that has yet to occur. In the latter case, responsiveness is anticipative, though the phrase may seem paradoxical.

Scanning: refers to a way of information acquisition when managers are involved in a sort of pre-attentive monitoring or exploration of information without any particular decision to take or question being identified to guide the research.

The objective is to be vigilant to discrepant signs/signals that might manifest in the peripheral vision and could eventually help identify, discover or anticipate plausible changes in the environment. Thus, information evaluation is both heuristic and inductive.

Sign: refers to a linguistic unity formed of a signaler and a signaled:

– The signaler refers to the sensitive part of the sign: that which a person perceives through his senses (a symbol, a shape, a color, a smell, etc.). It is either an emerging and spontaneous manifestation of nature, or an involuntary and unconscious manifestation of people's actions.

– The signaled, for its part, refers to the abstract part of the sign: the meaning that a person gives to the sensory perception, which, through convention, natural rapport or the association of ideas, takes the place of a reality that is absent, more complex. It has either a conventional meaning or a more subjective interpretation.

Signal: refers to a message that may come in various forms: quantitative or qualitative, linguistic or otherwise, written or spoken. It is deliberately and voluntarily emitted by a source that may be, depending on the case, a natural or a legal person, or alternatively a technical device. When a signal is emitted by a person without the latter's intention, or even awareness, this is preferably referred to as a "sign". For example, in a work meeting, a participant may start on hearing certain words. That start is a sign to those able to see it and interpret it.

Strategic decision: refers to a decision that shows the following characteristics:

– it is made in a situation of uncertainty, of incomplete information, in a complex environment, variable/mutating environment (as opposed to "all things being otherwise equal");

– it is not recurrent, therefore the decision maker is relatively deprived;

– it may have far-reaching (favorable or adverse) consequences that could jeopardize the survivability of the enterprise;

– it is systemic (many elements with many relationships among them);

– the decision maker does not have experience-proven models (one cannot resort to "turnkey" mechanisms).

Sustainable competitiveness: refers to the ability of an enterprise to maintain itself, durably and deliberately, in the competitive and evolving market of its choosing, while achieving a profit ratio at least equal to the ratio required for its activities to adapt and survive.

Target: refers to that part of the environment (*business environment*) that the enterprise wishes to put under surveillance. It comprises a list of agents in the environment and a list of topics (objects or events). The target is the result of the targeting operation. Scanning targeting is the operation that consists of delineating that part of the enterprise's external environment that is a common interest to potential users of the scanning information. Targeting is performed using the Target method and leads to the production of deliverables.

Topic: is a center of interest when considering the future of the organization.

Turbulence: denotes the fact that: "the dynamic properties [arise] not simply from the interaction of identifiable component systems but from the field itself (the "ground"). We call these environments turbulent fields. The turbulence results from the complexity and (multiplicity) of the causal interconnections..."[EME 65, p. 199].

Uncertainty: refers to the difference between the amount of information required to perform a given task, and the amount of information already possessed by the organization.

Vigilance: refers to:

– being alertly watchful for the detection of weak signals and discontinuities about emerging strategic threats and opportunities in the organizational environment;

– initiating further probing based on such detection.

Warning mode: refers to a way of searching for, and disseminating, anticipative information. The search is conducted without a very specific pointer. The gatekeeper has received no other instructions than being watchful, on the lookout, in a designated field, for any information whose interpretation might trigger a warning to his/her hierarchy. The potential user of the information does not formulate, *a priori*, a specific, detailed informational need.

Weak signal: refers to a decision-support "tool". This would appear, at first glance, as an unremarkable "data item," but its interpretation can trigger a warning. This warning indicates that an event may occur, possibly with considerable consequences (in terms of opportunity or threat). Upon interpretation, the signal is no longer referred to as weak, becoming instead an early warning signal.

Bibliography

[AGU 67] AGUILAR F.J., *Scanning the Business Environment*, Macmillan, New York, 1967.

[ALB 04] ALBRIGHT K.S., "Environmental scanning: radar for success", *The Information Management Journal*, vol. 38, no. 3, pp. 38–45, May–June 2004.

[ANS 75] ANSOFF H.I., "Managing strategic surprise by response to weak signals", *California Management Review*, vol. 18, no. 2, pp. 21–33, 1975.

[BAS 98] BASKERVILLE R.L., WOOD-HARPER, A.T., "Diversity in information systems action research methods", *European Journal of Information Systems*, vol. 7, no. 2, pp. 90–107, 1998.

[BAT 11] BATTISTELLA C., DE TONI A.F., "A methodology of technological foresight: a proposal and field study", *Technological Forecasting & Social Change*, vol. 78, no. 6, pp. 1029–1048, July 2011.

[BAW 99] BAWDEN D., HOLTHAM C., COURTNEY N., "Perspectives on information overload", *Aslib Proceedings*, vol. 51, no. 8, pp. 249–255, 1999.

[BE 13] Bulletins-Electronique.com, "Transition énergétique allemande : création d'une plateforme nationale de recherche", 7 March 2013. (http://www.bulletins-electroniques.com/actualites/72462.htm)

[BER 94] BERNHARDT D.C., "I want it fast, factual actionable – tailoring competitive intelligence to executives' needs", *Long Range Planning*, vol. 27, no. 1, pp. 12–24, February 1994.

[BER 13] BERNY L., THEVENIN L., VIDAL F., "Henri de Castries, PDG d'AXA: La France doit sortir du déni de réalité", *Les Echos*, no. 21427, p.18, 29 April 2013.

[BET 12] BETTIS-OUTLAND H., "Decision-making's impact on organizational learning and information overload", *Journal of Business Research*, vol. 65, no. 6, pp. 814–820, June 2012.

[BLA 03] BLANCO S., LESCA N., "From weak signals to anticipative information: learning from the implementation of an information selection method", in CASEBY D. (ed.), *In Search of Time: Proceedings of the International Conference* (ISIDA), Palermo, Italy, pp. 197–210, 8–10 May 2003.

[BOT 10] BOTTERHUIS L., VAN DER DUIN P., DE RUIJTER P., *et al.*, "Monitoring the future. Building an early warning system for the Dutch Ministry of Justice", *Futures*, vol. 42, no. 5, pp. 454–465, June 2010.

[CHO 01a] CHOO C.W., *Information Management for the Intelligent Organization: The Art of Scanning the Environment*, Information Today Inc., Medford, NJ, p. 325, 2001.

[CHO 01b] CHOO C.W., "Environmental scanning as information seeking and organizational learning", *Information Research*, vol. 7, no. 1, pp. 1–11, October 2001.

[CHO 09] CHOO C.W., "Information use and early warning effectiveness: perspectives and prospects", *Journal of the American Society for Information Science and Technology*, vol. 60, no. 5, pp. 1071–1082, 2009.

[DAF 86] DAFT R.L., LENGEL K.E., "Organizational information requirements, media richness and structural design", *Management Science*, vol. 32, no. 5, pp. 554–571, 1986.

[DAY 04] DAY G.S., SCHOEMAKER P.J.H., "Driving through the fog: managing at the edge", *Long Range Planning*, vol. 37, no. 2, pp. 127–142, April 2004.

[DAY 06] DAY G.S., SCHOEMAKER P.J.H., *Peripheral Vision: Detecting the Weak Signals that Will Make or Break Your Company*, Harvard Business School Press, Boston, MA, p. 248, 2006.

[DEC 05] DECKER R., WAGNER R., SCHOLZ S.W., "An internet-based approach to environmental scanning in marketing planning", *Marketing Intelligence & Planning*, vol. 23, no. 2, pp. 189–199, 2005.

[DER 11] DEREK D., WEBB C., "Recovering from information overload", *McKinsey Quarterly*, pp. 80–88, January 2011.

[EDM 00] EDMUNDS A., MORRIS A., "The problem of information overload in business organisations: a review of the literature", *International Journal of Information Management*, vol. 20, no. 1, pp. 17–28, February 2000.

[EIS 88] EISENHARDT K.M., BOURGEOIS L.J., "Politics of strategic decision making in high-velocity environments: toward a midrange theory", *The Academy of Management Journal*, vol. 32, no. 4, pp. 737–770, December 1988.

[EME 65] EMERY F.E., TRIST E.L., "The causal texture of organizational environments", *Human Relations*, vol. 18, no. 1, pp. 21–32, February 1965.

[FRE 84] FREEMAN R.E., *Strategic Management: A Stakeholder Approach*, Pitman, Boston, 1984.

[GIL 03] GILAD B., *Early Warning: Using Competitive Intelligence to Anticipate Market Shifts, Control Risk, and Create Powerful Strategies*, AMACOM, New York, NY, p. 272, 2003.

[HAM 81] HAMBRICK D.C., "Specialization of environmental scanning activities among upper level executives", *Journal of Management Studies*, vol. 18, no. 3, pp. 299–320, July 1981.

[HEI 12] HEINONEN S., HILTUNEN E., "Creative foresight space and the futures window: using visual weak signals to enhance anticipation and innovation", *Futures*, vol. 44, no. 3, pp. 248–56, April 2012.

[HEM 09] HEMP H., "Death by information overload", *Harvard Business Review*, vol. 87, no. 9, pp. 82–89, September 2009.

[HIL 06] HILTUNEN E., "Was it a wild card or just our blindness to gradual change?", *Journal of Futures Studies*, vol. 11, no. 2, pp. 61–74, November 2006.

[HIL 07] HILTUNEN E., "The futures window – a medium for presenting visual weak signals to trigger employees' futures thinking in organizations", *Working Paper w-423*, HSE Publications, London.

[HIL 08] HILTUNEN E., "Good sources of weak signals: a global study of where futurists look for weak signals", *Journal of Futures Studies*, vol. 12, no. 4, pp. 21–44, 2008.

[ILM 06] ILMOLA L., KUUSI O., "Filters of weak signals hinder foresight: monitoring weak signals efficiently in corporate decision-making", *Futures*, vol. 38, no. 8, pp. 908–924, October 2006.

[KÖN 07] KÖNNÖLÄ T., BRUMMER V., SALO A., "Diversity in foresight: insights from the fostering of innovation ideas", *Technological Forecasting & Social Change*, vol. 74, pp. 608–626, 2007.

[KUO 10] KUOSA T., "Futures signals sense-making framework (FSSF): a start-up tool to analyse and categorise weak signals, wild cards, drivers, trends and other types of information", *Futures*, vol. 42, no. 1, pp. 42–48, February 2010.

[KUO 11] KUOSA T., "Different approaches of pattern management and strategic intelligence", *Technological Forecasting & Social Change*, vol. 78, no. 3, pp. 458–467, March 2011.

[KUU 11] KUUSI O., HILTUNEN E., "The signification process of the future sign", *Journal of Futures Studies*, vol. 16, no. 1, pp. 47–66, September 2011.

[LAU 12] LAU R.Y.K., LIAO S.S., WONG K.F., *et al.*, "Web 2.0 environmental scanning and adaptative decision support for business mergers and acquisitions", *MIS Quarterly*, vol. 36, no. 4, pp. 1239–1268, December 2012.

[LES 11] LESCA H., LESCA N., *Weak Signals for Strategic Intelligence, Anticipation Tool for Managers*, ISTE Ltd, London, John Wiley & Sons, New York, p. 230, 2011.

[LES 12] LESCA N., CARON-FASAN M.-L., FALCY S., "How managers interpret scanning information", *Information & Management,* vol. 49, no. 2, pp. 126–134, March 2012.

[LI 11] LI T., LI M., "An investigation and analysis of information overload in manager's work", *iBusiness,* vol. 3, pp. 49–52, 2011.

[LIN 12] LIN H.-C., LUARN P., MAA R.-H., *et al.,* "Adaptive foresight modular design and dynamic adjustment mechanism: framework and Taiwan case study", *Technological Forecasting & Social Change,* vol. 79, no. 9, pp. 1583–1591, November 2012.

[LOZ 13] LOZA AGUIRE E., CARON-FASAN M.-L., LESCA N., *et al.,* "Using a meeting room system to improve targeting of environmental scanning", *Proceedings of the 15th IEEE Conference on Enterprise Systems,* Cape Town, South Africa, p. 10, 7–8 November 2013.

[MAL 96] MALTZ E., KOHLI A.L., "Market intelligence dissemination across functional boundaries", *Journal of Marketing Research,* vol. 33, no. 1, pp. 47–61, February 1996.

[MOS 11] MOSS KANTER R., "Zoom in, zoom out", *Harvard Business Review,* vol. 89, no. 3, pp. 112–116, March 2011.

[MOU 07] MOULTRIE J., NILSSON M., DISSEL M., *et al.,* "Innovation spaces: towards a framework for understanding the role of the physical environment in innovation", *Creativity and Innovation Management,* vol. 16, no. 1, pp. 53–65, March 2007.

[NEL 94] NELSON M.R., "We have the information you want, but getting it will cost you!: held hostage by information overload", *Crossroads,* vol. 1, no. 1, pp. 11–15, September 1994.

[OGI 13] OGIER T., "Le géant pétrolier Petrobras traverse une passe difficile", *Les Echos,* p.18, 14 May 2013.

[OVE 06] OVERBY O., BHARADWAJ. A, SAMBAMURTHY. V., "Enterprise agility and the enabling role of information technology", *European Journal of Information Systems,* vol. 15, pp. 120–131, 2006.

[PAR 13] PARASKEVAS A., ALTINAY L., "Signal detection as the first line of defence in tourism crisis management", *Tourism Management,* vol. 34, pp. 158–171, February 2013.

[QIU 08] QIU T., "Scanning for competitive intelligence: a managerial perspective", *European Journal of Marketing*, vol. 42, no. 7–8, pp. 814–835, 2008.

[ROH 11] ROHRBECK R., "Corporate foresight: its three roles in enhancing the innovation capacity of a firm", *Technological Forecasting & Social Change*, vol. 78, pp. 231–243, 2011.

[ROS 11] ROSSEL P., "Beyond the obvious: Examining ways of consolidating early detection schemes", *Technological Forecasting & Social Change*, vol. 78, no. 3, pp. 375–385, March 2011.

[ROS 12] ROSSEL P., "Early detection, warning, weak signals and seeds of change: a turbulent domain of futures studies", *Futures*, vol. 44, no. 3, pp. 229–239, April 2012.

[SCH 09] SCHOEMAKER P.J., DAY G.S., "How to make sense of weak signals", *MIT Sloan Management Review*, vol. 50, no. 3, pp. 81–89, Spring 2009.

[SCH 13a] SCHOEMAKER P.J., DAY G.S., SNYDER S.A., "Integrating organizational networks, weak signals, strategic radars and scenario planning", *Technological Forecasting & Social Change*, vol. 80, no. 4, pp. 815–824, May 2013.

[SCH 13b] SCHWARTZ J.O., KROEHL R, VON DER GRACHT H.A., "Novels and novelty in trend research: using novels to perceive weak signals and transfer frames of reference", *Technological Forecasting & Social Change*, 2013.

[STA 97] STANLEY A.J., CLIPSHAIN P.S., "Information overload: myth or reality?", *Communication of the IEEE Colloquium on IT Strategies for Information Overload*, London, pp. 1–4, 3 December 1997.

[STO 82] STOFFELS J.D., "Environmental scanning for future success", *Managerial Planning*, vol. 3, no. 3, pp. 4–12, 1982.

[THE 13] THÉRIN F., "Départ surprise du patron du géant suisse ABB", *Les Echos*, p.18, 13 May 2013.

[VAN 97] VANDENBOSH B., HUFF S.L., "Searching and scanning: how executives obtain information from executive information systems", *MIS Quarterly*, vol. 21, no. 1, pp. 81–108, 1997.

[WAL 92] WALLS J., WIDMEYER G.R., EL SAWY O.A., "Building an information system design theory for vigilant EIS", *Information System Research*, vol. 3, no. 1, pp. 36–59, March 1992.

[WAL 03] WALTERS B.A., JIANG J.J., KLEIN G., "Strategic information and strategic decision making: the EIS/CEO interface in smaller manufacturing", *Information & Management*, vol. 40, no. 6, pp. 487–495, July 2003.

[XU 11] XU M., ONG V., DUAN Y., *et al.*, "Intelligent agent systems for executive information scanning, filtering and interpretation: perceptions and challenges", *Information Processing and Management*, vol. 47, no. 2, pp. 186–201, March 2011.

[YOO 12] YOON J., "Detecting weak signals for long-term business opportunities using text mining of Web news", *Expert Systems with Applications*, vol. 39, no. 16, pp. 1243–12550, November 2012.

Index

Printed and bound by CPI Group (UK) Ltd, Croydon, CR0 4YY

27/10/2024

14580731-0005